PORN is not SEX ED!

of related interest

It's Totally Normal!
An LGBTQIA+ Guide to Puberty, Sex, and Gender
Monica and Asha Mehta
Illustrated by Fox Fisher
ISBN 978 1 83997 355 0
eISBN 978 1 83997 356 7

The Every Body Book of Consent
An LGBTQIA-Inclusive Guide to Respecting Boundaries, Bodies, and Beyond
Rachel Simon
Illustrated by Noah Grigni
ISBN 978 1 83997 683 4
eISBN 978 1 83997 684 1

How to Understand Your Sexuality
A Practical Guide to Exploring Who You Are
Meg-John Barker and Alex Iantaffi
Illustrated by Jules Scheele
Foreword by Erika Moen
ISBN 978 1 78775 618 2
eISBN 978 1 78775 619 9

First published in Great Britain in 2025
by Jessica Kingsley Publishers
An imprint of John Murray Press

1

Front cover image source: Remy Alva. The cover image is for illustrative purposes only, and any person featuring is a model.

This book contains mention of abuse, homophobia, pregnancy, sexual abuse, and transphobia.

A CIP catalogue record for this title is available from the British Library and the Library of Congress

ISBN 978 1 80501 325 9

Printed and bound in China by Leo Paper Products Ltd

Jessica Kingsley Publishers' policy is to use papers that are natural, renewable and recyclable products and made from wood grown in sustainable forests. The logging and manufacturing processes are expected to conform to the environmental regulations of the country of origin.

Jessica Kingsley Publishers
Carmelite House
50 Victoria Embankment
London EC4Y 0DZ

www.jkp.com

John Murray Press
Part of Hodder & Stoughton Ltd
An Hachette Company

The authorised representative in the EEA is Hachette Ireland, 8 Castlecourt Centre, Dublin 15, D15 XTP3, Ireland (email: info@hbgi.ie)

PORN is not SEX ED!

A YOUNG PERSON'S ILLUSTRATED GUIDE TO DEBUNKING SEXUALITY MYTHS

JESS MELENDEZ

ILLUSTRATED BY REMY ALVA

Jessica Kingsley Publishers
London and Philadelphia

TABLE OF CONTENTS

INTRODUCTION

HEY THERE! MY NAME IS ***JESS***, AND I'M A SEXUAL HEALTH EDUCATOR. AS AN EDUCATOR, I LIKE DISCUSSING TOPICS IMPORTANT TO OUR HEALTH, LIKE SEX AND SEXUALITY!

WELCOME TO A JOURNEY WHERE WE'RE GOING TO TACKLE A TOPIC THAT YOU MIGHT HAVE HEARD ABOUT BEFORE, AND FEELS A BIT AWKWARD DISCUSSING:

PORNOGRAPHY

EVER WONDER WHY SEX MAKES PEOPLE FEEL EMBARRASSED? EVEN THOUGH IT'S ALL OVER MOVIES, MUSIC, AND TV, OUR SOCIETY STILL ACTS LIKE IT'S A BIG SECRET. **BUT *WHY?*** MAYBE IT'S BECAUSE WE DON'T REALLY GET IT, OR BECAUSE WE FEEL LIKE WE'RE SUPPOSED TO BE EXPERTS WHEN WE'RE NOT.

WE'RE HERE TO CHANGE THAT! THIS BOOK IS ALL ABOUT *NORMALIZING THE CONVERSATION ABOUT PORN.*

BECAUSE WHEN WE TALK ABOUT STUFF THAT MAKES US UNCOMFORTABLE, THAT'S WHEN WE REALLY START TO LEARN AND GROW!

IN THIS BOOK, WE'RE GOING TO EXPLORE WHAT PORN IS ALL ABOUT AND HOW IT SHAPES OUR LIVES. WE'LL COVER EVERYTHING FROM BODY IMAGE TO CONSENT, SAFER SEX, AND MORE!!

THIS BOOK CONTAINS ACTIVITIES THAT ARE MEANT TO HELP YOU UNDERSTAND THE IMPACT OF PORN. YOU'LL ALSO SEE BOXES LABELED **"ASK YOUR ADULT"** ON SOME PAGES THAT CONTAIN QUESTIONS. THESE ARE MEANT TO SPARK CONVERSATIONS WITH A PARENT OR ANOTHER ADULT YOU TRUST. SOMETIMES TALKING WITH SOMEONE OLDER CAN HELP US UNDERSTAND THINGS BETTER.

ASK YOUR ADULT

ASK THESE QUESTIONS TO YOUR PARENT OR TRUSTED ADULT

PORN IS SOMETHING THAT IS CONSIDERED A COMMUNITY HEALTH TOPIC, WHICH MEANS THAT IT IS A TOPIC THAT AFFECTS NOT ONLY YOU BUT PEOPLE IN YOUR COMMUNITY. ONE STUDY SHOWED THAT NEARLY 3 IN 4 TEENS (73%) HAVE BEEN EXPOSED TO PORNOGRAPHY, EITHER ACCIDENTALLY OR ON PURPOSE.* IT'S MORE COMMON THAN WE THINK AND IMPORTANT TO KNOW HOW IT HAS A ROLE IN OUR LIVES.

LET'S START THIS JOURNEY TOGETHER!

*ROBB, M.B., & MANN, S. (2023). TEENS AND PORNOGRAPHY. SAN FRANCISCO, CA: COMMON SENSE.

CHECK THE BOX

TAKE A LOOK AT THIS LIST OF STATEMENTS.
CHECK THE BOX FOR EVERY STATEMENT THAT APPLIES TO YOU.

DO YOU...

- [ ] HAVE ACCESS TO THE INTERNET ON YOUR PHONE?
- [ ] HAVE ACCESS TO THE INTERNET AT YOUR HOME?
- [ ] KNOW SOMEONE WHO HAS RECEIVED A SEXT BEFORE? *(**SEXT**: A SEXY/FLIRTY TEXT MESSAGE)*
- [ ] KNOW SOMEONE WHO HAS WATCHED PORN BEFORE?
- [ ] KNOW SOMEONE WHO HAS RESTRICTIONS ON THEIR USE OF MEDIA?
- [ ] FOLLOW ANY MAKE-UP, BEAUTY, OR FITNESS PAGES ON SOCIAL MEDIA?

HAVE YOU EVER...

- [ ] SEARCHED INFORMATION ONLINE INSTEAD OF ASKING SOMEONE?
- [ ] LOOKED UP SOMETHING OUT OF CURIOSITY?
- [ ] BEEN TOLD TO NOT BELIEVE EVERYTHING YOU SEE ON THE INTERNET?
- [ ] HAD AN ADVERTISMENT POP UP ON YOUR FEED?
- [ ] SEEN A PICTURE OR VIDEO THAT WAS ALTERED IN SOME WAY?
- [ ] ALTERED A PHOTO?

FOLLOW-UP:

DID ANY OF THESE STATEMENTS STAND OUT TO YOU? ____________________

WHAT DID ALL OF THESE STATEMENTS HAVE IN COMMON? ____________________

____

____

____

____

____

THE QUESTIONS IN THIS ACTIVITY ARE TO PREPARE YOU FOR THE TOPICS COVERED IN THIS BOOK. THIS BOOK INTENDS TO GUIDE YOU TO START DISCUSSING MEDIA AND SEXUALITY. IF YOU DON'T, WHO WILL?

1

THIS CHAPTER WILL HELP BREAK DOWN THE DEFINITION OF PORNOGRAPHY AND WHERE IT CAME FROM.

ONCE YOU COMPLETE THIS CHAPTER, FIND YOUR TRUSTED ADULT TO TALK TO AND ASK ANY QUESTIONS YOU HAVE.

WHAT COMES TO YOUR MIND WHEN YOU HEAR THE WORD

PORN!

WHAT QUESTIONS DO YOU HAVE ABOUT PORN?

THINK OF A YOUNG PERSON IN YOUR LIFE:

A SIBLING, COUSIN, FRIEND, OR NEIGHBOR.

YOU ARE SOMEONE THEY TRUST AND ALWAYS ASK FOR ADVICE.

ONE DAY THEY COME UP TO YOU AND ASK,

WHAT'S **PORN**?

I HEARD ABOUT IT AT SCHOOL TODAY.

HOW WOULD YOU RESPOND?

HOW WOULD *YOU* **DEFINE PORN**?

SEEMS TRICKY, RIGHT?

HOW ON EARTH DO YOU EXPLAIN PORN TO SOMEONE WHO IS SO MUCH YOUNGER THAN YOU?

IN SOCIETY, WE SEE A LOT OF MEDIA THAT IS SEXUALIZED, MEANING TO TAKE A PERSON, SITUATION, OR PLACE AND MAKE IT SEEM SEXUAL. PEOPLE SOMETIMES CALL THIS "SEXUALLY EXPLICIT."

THIS APPLIES TO ALL GENDERS.

WE MIGHT NOT EVEN NOTICE IT BECAUSE OF HOW FREQUENT AND NORMAL IT SEEMS.

SOMETIMES IT CAN BE DIFFICULT FOR US TO UNDERSTAND WHAT IS CONSIDERED SEXUALLY EXPLICIT AND WHAT IS NOT.

WHEN WAS THE FIRST TIME YOU HEARD ABOUT PORN?

CIRCLE YOUR ANSWER:

HIGH SCHOOL

MIDDLE SCHOOL

ELEMENTARY SCHOOL

OTHER

LIST SOME REASONS WHY THIS MAY BE A TOPIC THAT FEW PEOPLE DISCUSS.

____

____

____

____

____

____

HOW CAN SOMEONE ACCESS PORN? IS IT EASY? IS IT DIFFICULT?

____

____

____

____

____

____

SIMILAR TO SEX AND SEXUALITY, SOCIETY VIEWS PORN AS A CONTROVERSIAL TOPIC. WE MAY SEE IT BEING SHOWN IN THE MEDIA FREQUENTLY, BUT WE DON'T TALK ABOUT IT FOR SOME REASON. ONCE AGAIN, THIS BOOK INTENDS TO CREATE AWARENESS BY *NORMALIZING* THE CONVERSATION ABOUT PORN.

NORMALIZING SEX

WORD SEARCH PUZZLE

THIS WORD SEARCH INCLUDES WORDS RELATED TO SEX AND SEXUALITY. TO SOME, THESE WORDS SEEM "INAPPROPRIATE OR NAUGHTY." NOT TODAY! THERE IS NOTHING WRONG WITH USING THESE WORDS OR WANTING TO LEARN ABOUT THEM. HOW MANY OF THESE WORDS DO YOU KNOW?

C V A G I N A L F L U I D S V A F N V C
P U Z M J R T N A C I R B U L O I A E L
Z S E X W O R K Q K E G W O R P G D P S
H B O J E Z A G E L A M Z E P I G J X J
M D K E S A F E R S E X S L N A I C O Q
T I K H W T M B A R C K E A A V L U V D
Q A S C I R C U M C I S E F K X X D S C
A A B O U Z A F F N Q Z R A G T E K P O
M T B O G U X D M S Y S I N E P N S O M
A I R C O Y J R Z F E T I S H I Z E R M
S Y E F Y B N X B S E M E N X W A Y N U
T D A K F O E Y E K F K F C C I V P N N
U M S E V I T A M R O N O R E T E H E I
R T T X F I A R I A H C I B U P A D B C
B I R H A M V W E F R T N E S N O C T A
A M Y A Q Y X D O S N C Y Y X L C Z Q T
T C E J N C O N D O M M X E S R E T N I
I K N T I S R G U J G D L O Y O D S X O
O O I L M A E R T S N I A M A M I T Z N
N Z C C H U M A N T R A F F I C K I N G

CAN YOU FIND THESE WORDS:

(WORDS GO HORIZONTALLY, VERTICALLY, DIAGONALLY, BACKWARDS AND FORWARDS)

CIS
TRANS
VULVA
PENIS
PORN
SEX
SAFER SEX
SEX WORK

INTERSEX
NIPPLE
TABOO
SEMEN
BREAST
CONDOM
LUBRICANT

VAGINA
CONSENT
FORESKIN
MALE GAZE
MISOGYNY
CIRCUMCISE
MASTURBATION

FETISHIZE
PUBIC HAIR
MAINSTREAM
VAGINAL FLUIDS
COMMUNICATION
HETERONORMATIVE
HUMAN TRAFFICKING

*DEFINITIONS IN BACK OF BOOK

2

THIS CHAPTER DISCUSSES WHY A PERSON MAY CHOOSE TO WATCH PORNOGRAPHY.

IT WILL ALSO INCLUDE A SENSITIVE HEALTH TOPIC CALLED "THE MALE GAZE."

REMEMBER, PORN IS A FORM OF ENTERTAINMENT CREATED FOR ADULTS.

ONCE YOU COMPLETE THIS CHAPTER, FIND YOUR TRUSTED ADULT TO TALK TO AND ASK ANY QUESTIONS YOU HAVE.

SOME REASONS ARE...

DURING MASTURBATION

MASTURBATION IS WHEN SOMEONE TOUCHES THEIR OWN BODY TO EXPERIENCE PLEASURE.

IT IS A HEALTHY AND SAFE WAY OF EXPLORING YOUR BODY. SOME PEOPLE MIGHT USE PORNOGRAPHY TO MAKE THEMSELVES FEEL SEXUALLY EXCITED.

TO EXPLORE SEXUAL FANTASY

IT IS NORMAL FOR ANYONE TO FANTASIZE ABOUT SEX. IT'S ALSO NORMAL FOR PEOPLE TO NOT. LIKE OTHER FORMS OF MEDIA, PORN OFFERS UP FANTASIES. FANTASY IS ALL ABOUT EXPLORING OUR IMAGINATION, WHERE THERE ARE NO LIMITS TO WHAT WE CAN DO.

TO USE WITH A PARTNER

SOMETIMES WHEN WE FIND SOMETHING EXCITING, WE WANT TO SHARE IT WITH SOMEONE ELSE. IN A RELATIONSHIP, SOME PEOPLE MIGHT BE CURIOUS ABOUT WATCHING PORN TOGETHER.

IT'S IMPORTANT TO REMEMBER THAT EVERYONE INVOLVED HAS TO GIVE **CONSENT**,

WHICH MEANS GIVING **PERMISSION**.

TO ANSWER QUESTIONS ABOUT SEX AND SEXUALITY

THINK ABOUT YOUR EXPERIENCE IN SCHOOL. DO YOU HAVE A CLASS THAT TEACHES SEXUAL HEALTH? MANY STUDENTS LIVING IN THE UNITED STATES DO NOT.

PORN IS A TOOL THAT SOME PEOPLE HAVE USED TO LEARN ABOUT SEX.

PORN IS NOT SEX EDUCATION AND SHOULDN'T BE MISTAKEN FOR IT.

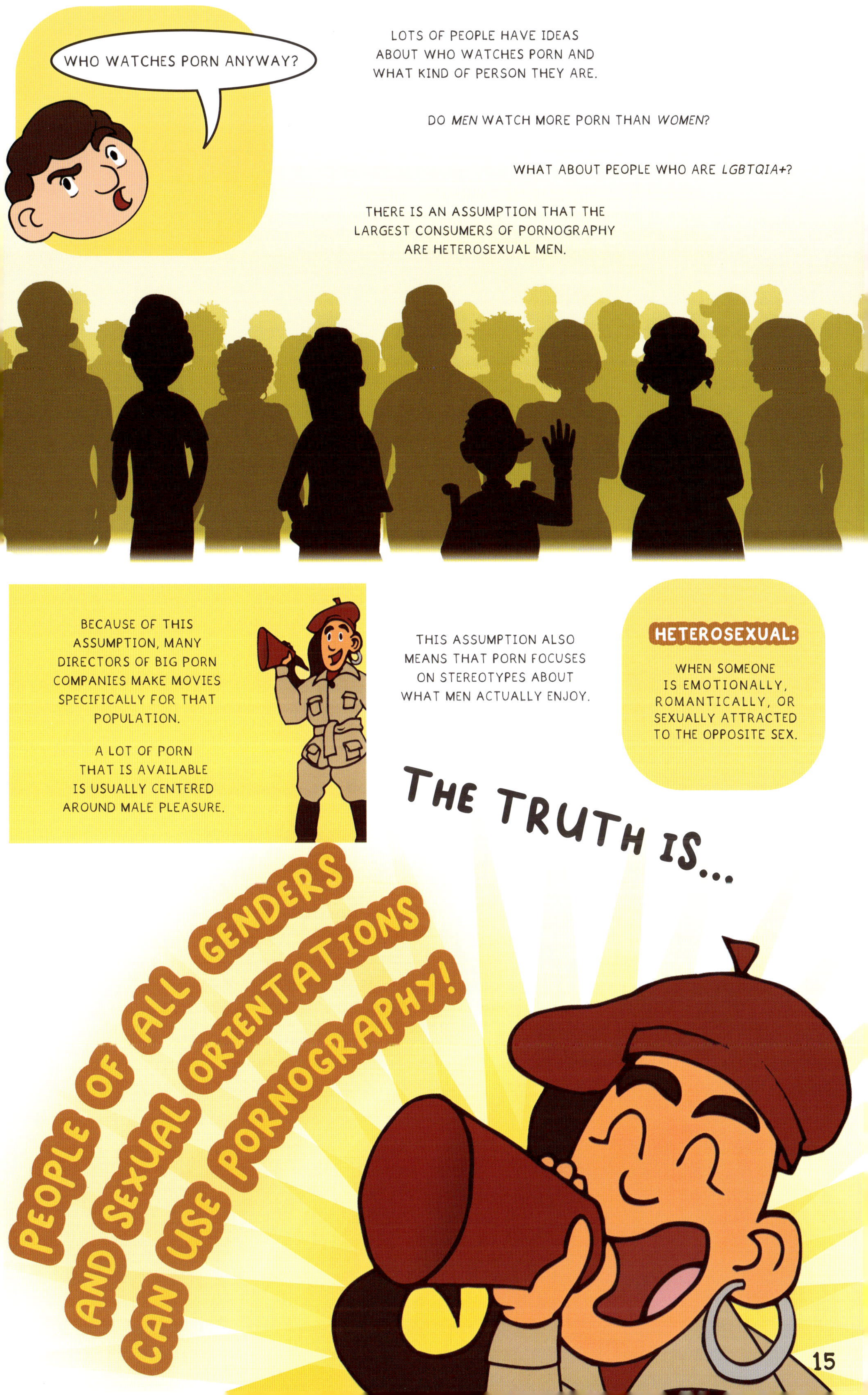

LOTS OF PEOPLE HAVE IDEAS ABOUT WHO WATCHES PORN AND WHAT KIND OF PERSON THEY ARE.

DO *MEN* WATCH MORE PORN THAN *WOMEN*?

WHAT ABOUT PEOPLE WHO ARE *LGBTQIA+*?

THERE IS AN ASSUMPTION THAT THE LARGEST CONSUMERS OF PORNOGRAPHY ARE HETEROSEXUAL MEN.

BECAUSE OF THIS ASSUMPTION, MANY DIRECTORS OF BIG PORN COMPANIES MAKE MOVIES SPECIFICALLY FOR THAT POPULATION.

A LOT OF PORN THAT IS AVAILABLE IS USUALLY CENTERED AROUND MALE PLEASURE.

THIS ASSUMPTION ALSO MEANS THAT PORN FOCUSES ON STEREOTYPES ABOUT WHAT MEN ACTUALLY ENJOY.

HETEROSEXUAL:

WHEN SOMEONE IS EMOTIONALLY, ROMANTICALLY, OR SEXUALLY ATTRACTED TO THE OPPOSITE SEX.

THE TRUTH IS...

PEOPLE OF ALL GENDERS AND SEXUAL ORIENTATIONS CAN USE PORNOGRAPHY!

QUICK FACTS ABOUT PORN:

PORN SITES RECEIVE MORE REGULAR MONTHLY TRAFFIC THAN NETFLIX, INSTAGRAM, AND TIKTOK.

THAT IS MORE THAN THE NUMBER OF PEOPLE BINGE-WATCHING THEIR FAVORITE SHOWS AND DOING TIKTOK CHALLENGES!

SOMETIMES PEOPLE ARE EXPOSED ACCIDENTALLY THROUGH THEIR ONLINE SEARCHES OR POP-UP ADS.

ACTIVITY TIME!

LET'S TALK ABOUT MEDIA AND GENDER REPRESENTATION.

ANSWER THE FOLLOWING QUESTIONS:

HOW DOES THE MEDIA PORTRAY WOMEN?

WHAT ARE SOME SONGS YOU HAVE HEARD ABOUT WOMEN, AND WHAT WAS THEIR MAIN MESSAGE?

WHAT MESSAGES HAVE CELEBRITIES OR INFLUENCERS GIVEN ABOUT WOMEN?

FOR WOMEN, DOES THE MEDIA FOCUS ON CERTAIN CHARACTERISTICS MORE THAN OTHERS?

ASK YOUR ADULT

HOW WERE GIRLS AND WOMEN SHOWN IN THE MEDIA WHEN YOU WERE YOUNGER?

ARE THINGS DIFFERENT NOW?

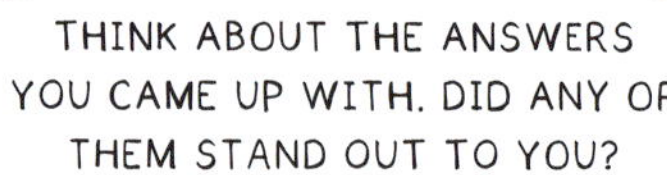

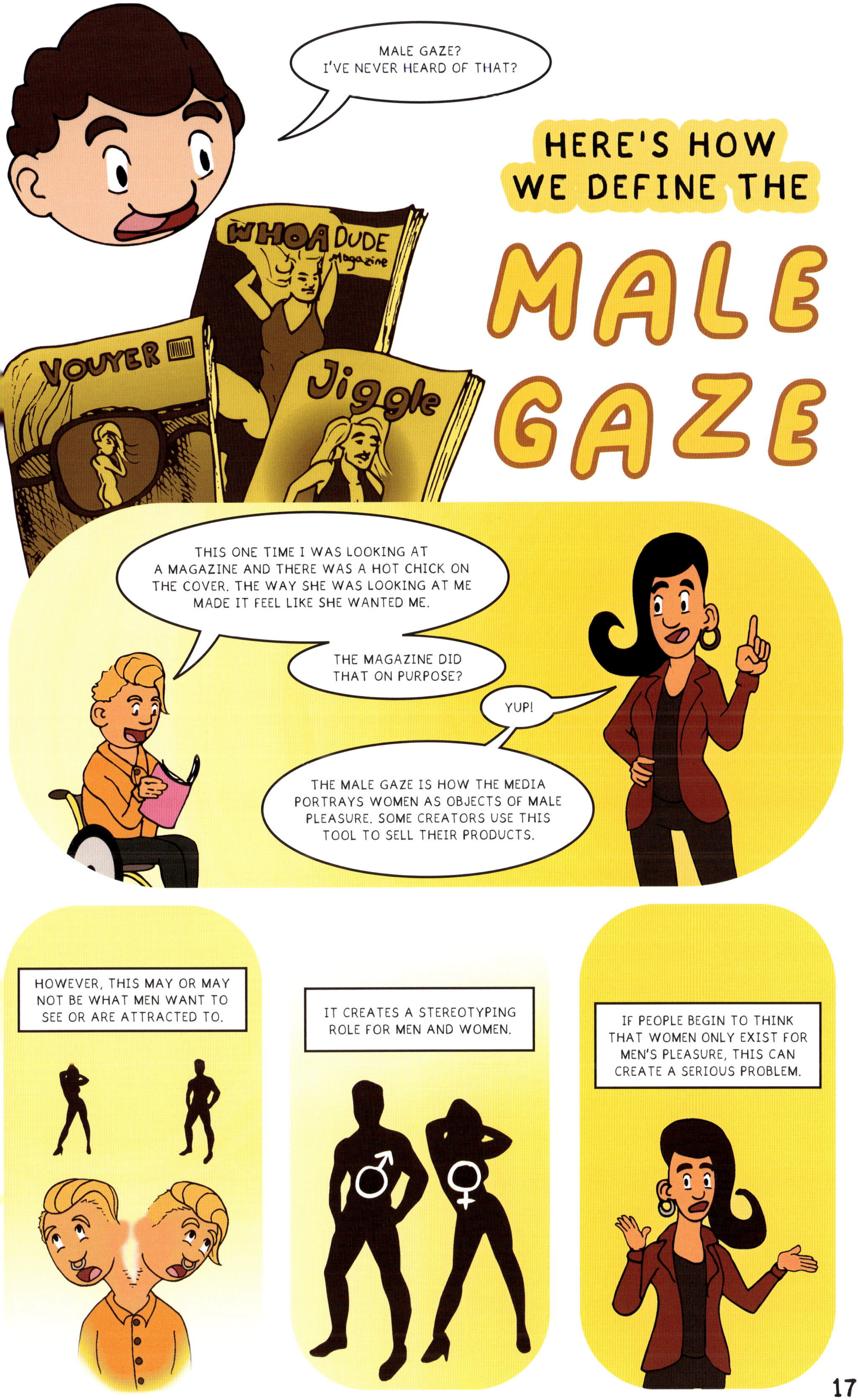

MALE GAZE?
I'VE NEVER HEARD OF THAT?

HERE'S HOW WE DEFINE THE MALE GAZE

WHOA DUDE Magazine

VOUYER

Jiggle

THIS ONE TIME I WAS LOOKING AT A MAGAZINE AND THERE WAS A HOT CHICK ON THE COVER. THE WAY SHE WAS LOOKING AT ME MADE IT FEEL LIKE SHE WANTED ME.

THE MAGAZINE DID THAT ON PURPOSE?

YUP!

THE MALE GAZE IS HOW THE MEDIA PORTRAYS WOMEN AS OBJECTS OF MALE PLEASURE. SOME CREATORS USE THIS TOOL TO SELL THEIR PRODUCTS.

WHAT IS A STEREOTYPE?

WHAT IS A GENDER STEREOTYPE?

BELIEFS ABOUT WHAT MEN AND WOMEN ARE LIKE AND WHAT TRAITS AND BEHAVIORS ARE EXPECTED OF THEM.

AND REMEMBER, THERE ARE MORE GENDERS THAN JUST WOMEN AND MEN.

WRITE DOWN SOME STEREOTYPES YOU HAVE HEARD ABOUT GENDER BELOW:

WOMEN	MEN

HOW MIGHT THESE IDEAS IMPACT HOW SOMEONE SEES THEMSELVES?

____

____

____

____

HOW DOES THIS AFFECT TRANSGENDER AND NON-BINARY FOLKS?

____

____

____

____

HOW CAN THE MALE GAZE AND STEREOTYPING BE HARMFUL?

THE MALE GAZE NEGATIVELY AFFECTS HOW WOMEN ARE SEEN. IT CAN MAKE WOMEN FEEL BAD ABOUT THEMSELVES, OR THINK THAT THEY NEED TO CHANGE HOW THEY LOOK IN ORDER TO BE ATTRACTIVE.

PLUS, WITH ALL THOSE FILTER APPS, IT'S MAKING BEAUTY STANDARDS IMPOSSIBLE TO REACH.

THE **MALE GAZE** REINFORCES STEREOTYPES BY PORTRAYING WOMEN AS OBJECTS FOR MEN'S ENJOYMENT, RATHER THAN BEING THEIR OWN PERSON WITH IDEAS AND GOALS.

HOW CAN WE CHALLENGE THE MALE GAZE?

PROMOTE GENDER DIVERSITY!

VALUE WOMEN FOR WHO THEY ARE, NOT HOW THEY LOOK

YOU LOOK SO PRETTY!

YOU HAVE GREAT IDEAS!

WRITE YOUR ANSWER BELOW:

3

BODY IMAGE

THIS CHAPTER TALKS ABOUT HOW PORNOGRAPHY REPRESENTS DIFFERENT BODIES. IT WILL ALSO INCLUDE A SENSITIVE HEALTH TOPIC CALLED "FETISHIZATION."

ONCE YOU COMPLETE THIS CHAPTER, FIND YOUR TRUSTED ADULT TO TALK TO AND ASK ANY QUESTIONS YOU HAVE.

INSIDE THE CIRCLE, WRITE DOWN WHAT COMES TO MIND WHEN YOU HEAR THE TERM "BODY IMAGE." IT CAN BE A SENTENCE, WORDS, PICTURE, ETC.

SEVERAL THINGS CAN COME TO MIND WHEN WE'RE THINKING ABOUT BODY IMAGE.

HERE ARE THREE WAYS TO DEFINE IT:

HOW YOU FEEL ABOUT YOUR BODY

YOUR PERCEPTION OF YOUR BODY

HOW YOU THINK OTHERS PERCEIVE YOUR BODY

LET'S TAKE A LOOK AT THAT WORD:

PERCEPTION

IMAGINE THAT YOU HAVE AN INVISIBLE PAIR OF SUNGLASSES.

THE SUNGLASSES THAT YOU LOOK THROUGH ARE CONSIDERED YOUR UNIQUE LENS.

HERE'S THE THING. NOBODY IN THE WORLD HAS THE SAME LENS THAT YOU DO.

MEN ARE SHOWN AS...

- PHYSICALLY FIT
- MUSCULAR
- HAVING LITTLE TO NO BODY HAIR
- HAVING A BIG PENIS
- DOMINANT

WOMEN ARE SHOWN AS...

- PHYSICALLY FIT
- HAVING NO BODY HAIR
- HAVING LARGE BREASTS
- HAVING A LARGE BUTT
- WEARING LOTS OF MAKE-UP

THE BODIES SHOWN IN PORN DO NOT REFLECT THE PEOPLE WHO EXIST IN OUR COMMUNITIES. THE INDUSTRY HIRES PERFORMERS FOR THE WAY THAT THEY LOOK.

QUESTION: IF THESE ARE THE ONLY TYPES OF BODIES A PERSON SEES IN PORN, DO YOU THINK THIS MIGHT AFFECT HOW SOMEONE SEES THEIR BODY? EXPLAIN.

IN PORN, FETISHIZING SOMEONE MEANS FOCUSING SEXUAL DESIRE ON SPECIFIC PARTS OF A PERSON.

IT CAN INCLUDE SOMEONE'S RACE, GENDER, BODY APPEARANCE, AND SEXUAL ORIENTATION.

FETISHIZING A PERSON'S IDENTITY IS **PROBLEMATIC**. SOMEONE IS NOW AN OBJECT RATHER THAN A WHOLE, COMPLEX PERSON.

THIS TYPE OF PORN REDUCES PEOPLE TO THINGS LIKE:

THEIR GENITAL SIZES OR THE TYPE OF GENITALS A PERSON HAS.

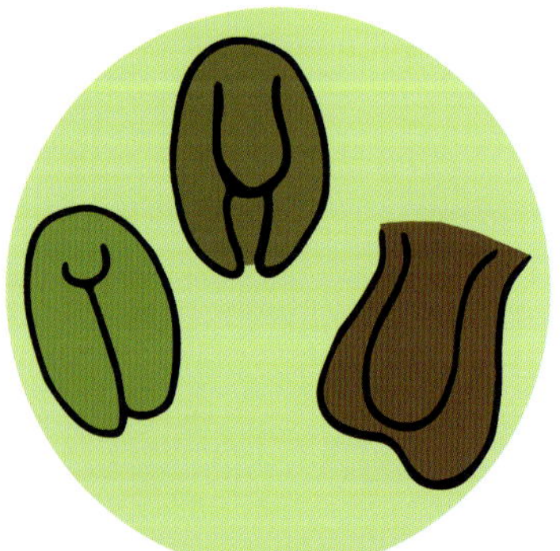

TRANSGENDER IDENTITIES

BODY SHAPE AND SIZE.

COLOR OF THEIR SKIN

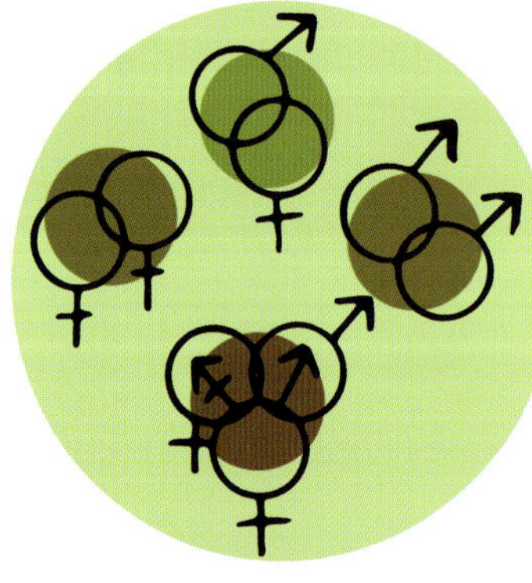

SEXUAL ORIENTATION

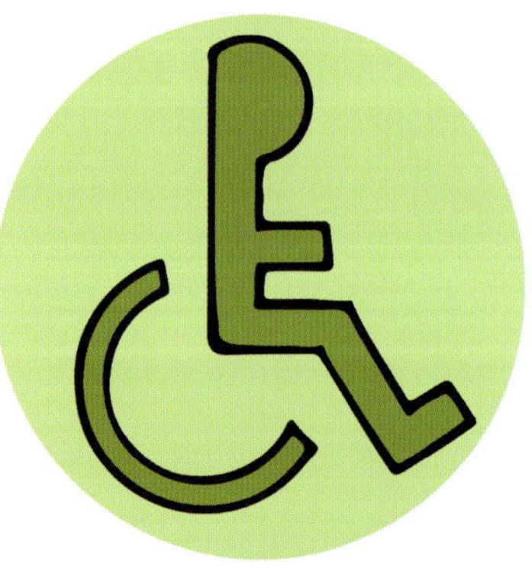

THEIR INTELLECTUAL OR PHYSICAL ABILITIES

THERE IS A DIFFERENCE BETWEEN APPRECIATING SOMEONE'S IDENTITY AND FETISHIZING THEM. IT IS PROBLEMATIC IN PORN BECAUSE IT CAN LEAD TO STEREOTYPING AND DISCRIMINATION.

TAKE A LOOK AT THE ACTIVITY BELOW. THIS FLOWCHART CAN HELP IDENTIFY THE DIFFERENCE BETWEEN THE TWO.

ATTRACTION OR FETISHIZING?

ARE YOU GENUINELY ATTRACTED TO THIS PERSON?

YES

IS IT BECAUSE OF THEIR RACE, AGE, IMMIGRATION STATUS, BODY SIZE, GENDER IDENTITY, OR CULTURE?

YES

IS IT BECAUSE THEY FIT A STEREOTYPE?

YES

IT'S TIME TO RETHINK WHY YOU ARE ATTRACTED TO THIS PERSON. BEING ATTRACTED TO SOMEONE SOLELY BASED ON STEREOTYPES IS CONSIDERED FETISHIZING A PERSON.

NO

NO

IS IT BECAUSE THEY ARE BEAUTIFUL IN THEIR OWN WAY?

YES

NO

NO

ARE YOU STILL INTERESTED IN PURSUING THEM?

YES

NO

IF YOU'RE NOT INTERESTED IN THAT PERSON, THAT'S OKAY. IT SEEMS LIKE THEY'RE JUST NOT THE RIGHT ONE FOR YOU.

DO YOU HAVE AN INTEREST IN LEARNING ABOUT WHAT THEIR CULTURE OR LIFE IS LIKE?

YES

GREAT! UNDERSTANDING THAT WE ALL COME FROM DIFFERENT BACKGROUNDS AND IDENTITIES IS IMPORTANT. RESPECTING OTHERS IS INCLUDED IN OUR ATTRACTION.

NO

HERE IS AN OPPORTUNITY TO RETHINK YOUR PURPOSE IN PURSUING SOMEONE. IS IT A *HOOKUP*? DO YOU WANT TO *DATE* THIS PERSON?

REMEMBER, PEOPLE ARE NOT OBJECTS. WE DON'T WANT TO REDUCE THEM TO CERTAIN PARTS OF THEIR IDENTITY. THAT IS CONSIDERED FETISHIZING.

BODY IMAGE REFLECTIONS

TAKE A MOMENT TO REVIEW THE QUESTIONS BELOW, FOCUSING ON YOUR BODY IMAGE. ANSWER EACH QUESTION HONESTLY AND OPENLY, KNOWING THAT YOUR THOUGHTS AND FEELINGS ARE AN OPPORTUNITY FOR SELF-REFLECTION AND GROWTH.

ONCE FINISHED, DISCUSS YOUR ANSWERS WITH A TRUSTED ADULT. USE THE PROMPT BELOW TO GAIN INSIGHT INTO THEIR EXPERIENCES WITH BODY IMAGE.

HOW DOES MEDIA INFLUENCE YOUR PERCEPTION OF YOUR BODY IMAGE?

WHAT DO YOU THINK ABOUT THE UNREALISTIC STANDARDS OF APPEARANCE PORTRAYED IN MEDIA? HOW DO THEY MAKE YOU FEEL ABOUT YOUR OWN BODY?

WHAT STRATEGIES CAN YOU USE TO FEEL GOOD ABOUT YOUR BODY WHEN FACED WITH NEGATIVE MEDIA MESSAGES?

WHAT DOES A POSITIVE BODY IMAGE MEAN TO YOU?

ASK YOUR ADULT

WHAT WAS IT LIKE FOR YOU WHEN YOU WERE MY AGE AND FIGURING OUT HOW YOU FELT ABOUT YOUR BODY?

HOW DO YOU THINK THE MEDIA'S MESSAGES ABOUT WHAT IS ATTRACTIVE HAVE CHANGED THROUGHOUT THE YEARS?

WHAT ADVICE WOULD YOU GIVE ME TO FEEL GOOD ABOUT MY BODY IMAGE?

MIRROR COMPLIMENTS

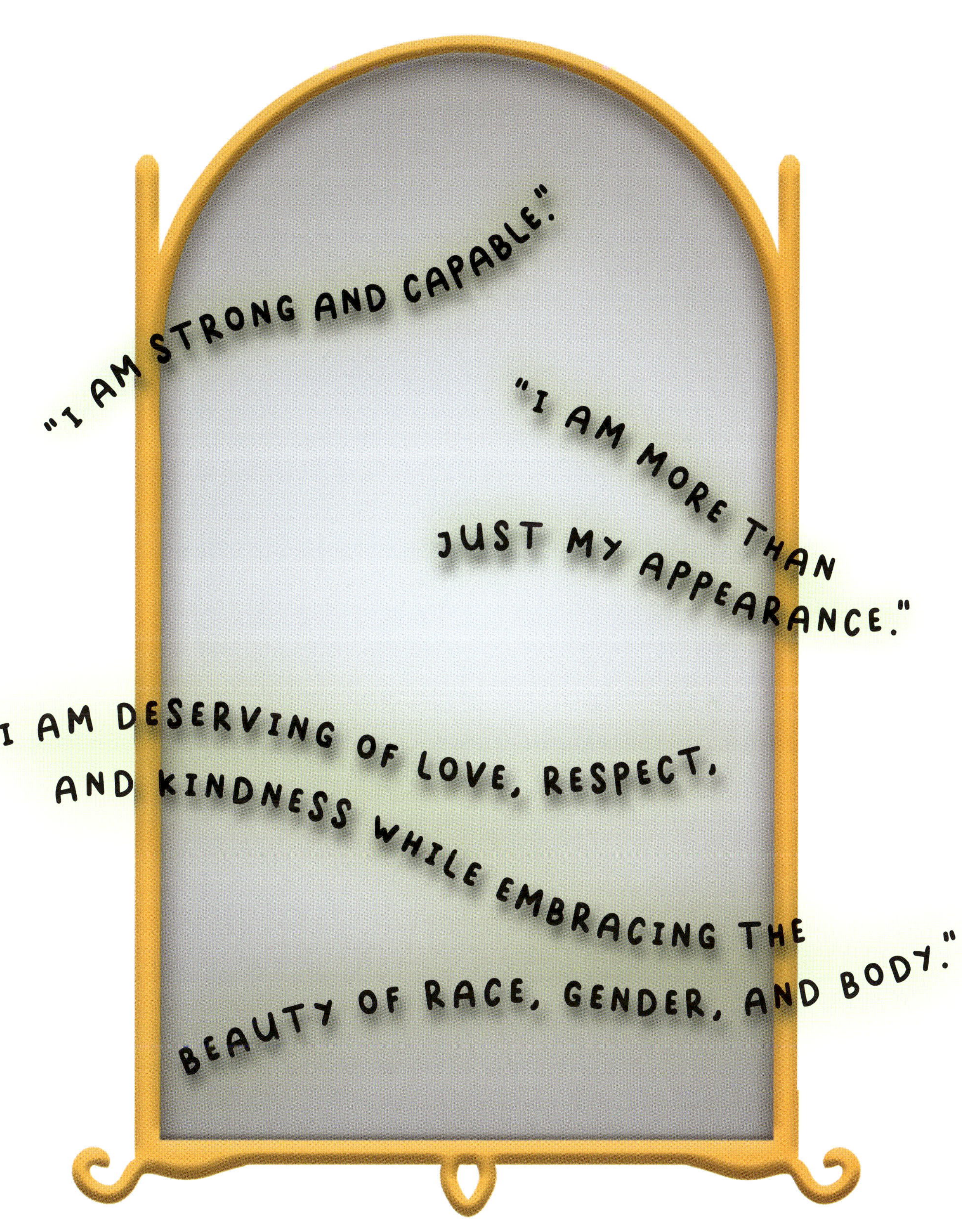

AFFIRMATIONS ARE SPECIAL POSITIVE WORDS OR PHRASES YOU SAY TO YOURSELF, LIKE A POWERFUL PEP TALK, TO HELP YOU FEEL CONFIDENT, STRONG, AND HAPPY ABOUT WHO YOU ARE. STAND IN FRONT OF A MIRROR AND WRITE AFFIRMATIONS DIRECTLY ON THE WORKSHEET INCLUDING THOUGHTS AND FEELINGS ABOUT YOUR BODY. REFLECT ON WHAT EACH AFFIRMATION MEANS TO YOU PERSONALLY.

4

THIS CHAPTER TALKS ABOUT ANATOMY AND HOW OUR BODIES EXPERIENCE PLEASURE.

THERE WILL BE IMAGES OF GENITALS FOR EDUCATIONAL PURPOSES.

ONCE YOU COMPLETE THIS CHAPTER, FIND YOUR TRUSTED ADULT TO TALK TO AND ASK ANY QUESTIONS YOU HAVE.

IN PORN, IT IS COMMON FOR GENITAL APPEARANCE TO BE ALTERED FOR FILM BY:

THE LAST CHAPTER DISCUSSED HOW MOST PORN DISPLAYS CERTAIN BODY TYPES. IN ADDITION TO BODIES, THE GENITALS SHOWN IN PORN ARE ALSO PARTICULAR IN THEIR APPEARANCE AND FUNCTION.

UNFORTUNATELY, THERE IS A LOT OF MISREPRESENTATION OF WHAT THESE BODY PARTS LOOK LIKE AND HOW THEY FUNCTION.

LET'S DIVE INTO A QUICK LITTLE ANATOMY LESSON

THE PENIS

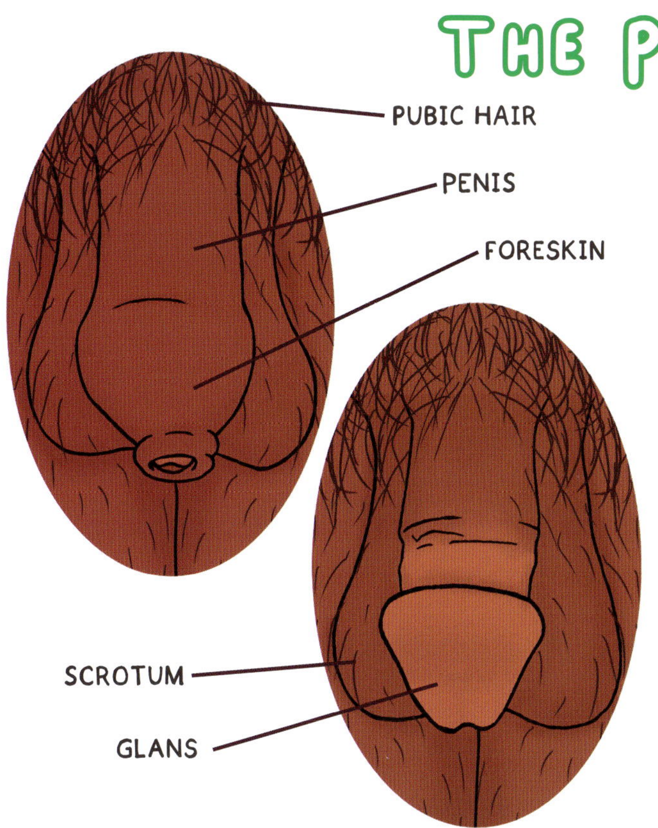

PUBIC HAIR - PROVIDES A CUSHION AGAINST FRICTION, HELPING PROTECT THE GENITALS FROM IRRITATION.

PENIS - LINED WITH PLEASURE-SENSITIVE NERVE ENDINGS AND MADE UP OF SPONGY TISSUE THAT FILLS UP WITH BLOOD WHEN AROUSED (SEXUALLY EXCITED). THIS IS ALSO THE TUBE WHERE URINE AND SPERM EXIT THROUGH.

FORESKIN - A LAYER OF SKIN THAT PROTECTS AND COVERS THE GLANS OF THE PENIS.

CIRCUMCISION - A SURGERY WHERE THE FORESKIN IS CUT FROM THE PENIS, EXPOSING THE GLANS. THIS IS DONE DURING INFANCY OR AS AN ADULT. PEOPLE HAVE THIS PROCEDURE FOR DIFFERENT CULTURAL OR APPEARANCE REASONS.

SCROTUM - HOLDS THE TESTICLES WHERE SPERM DEVELOPS. THE SCROTUM MOVES CLOSER OR FURTHER AWAY FROM THE BODY TO KEEP THE TESTICLES AT THE RIGHT TEMPERATURE. IF IT'S HOT, IT WILL MOVE AWAY FROM THE BODY (SOMETIMES LOOKING BIGGER). IF IT'S TOO COLD, IT WILL PULL CLOSER TO THE BODY (SOMETIMES LOOKING SMALLER).

GLANS - THE HEAD OR TIP OF THE PENIS. THIS IS TYPICALLY THE MOST SENSITIVE PART OF THE PENIS.

QUICK FACTS ABOUT THE PENIS

- SOME PENISES ARE CIRCUMCISED, AND SOME ARE NOT. A CIRCUMCISED PENIS IS JUST AS HEALTHY AS A NON-CIRCUMCISED PENIS.
- THERE IS NO BONE INSIDE THE PENIS!

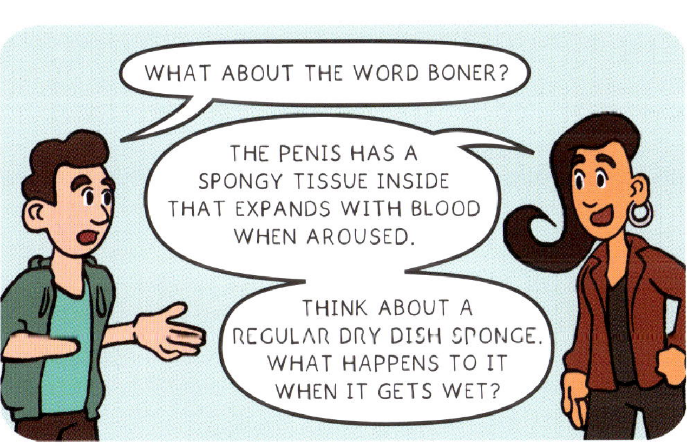

SPERM AND EJACULATION

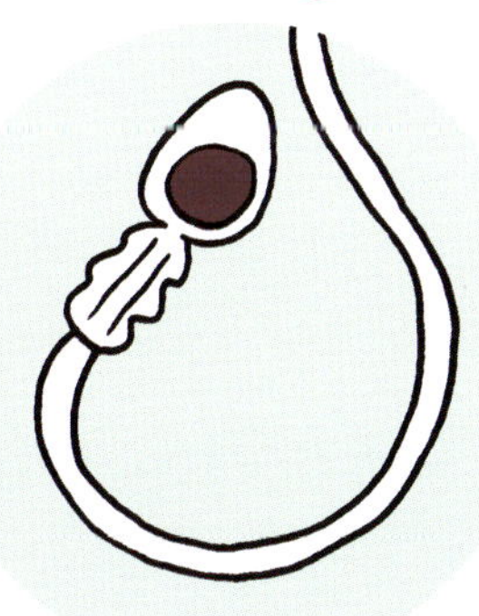

SPERM

A REPRODUCTIVE CELL; LOOKS LIKE A TADPOLE UNDER A MICROSCOPE.

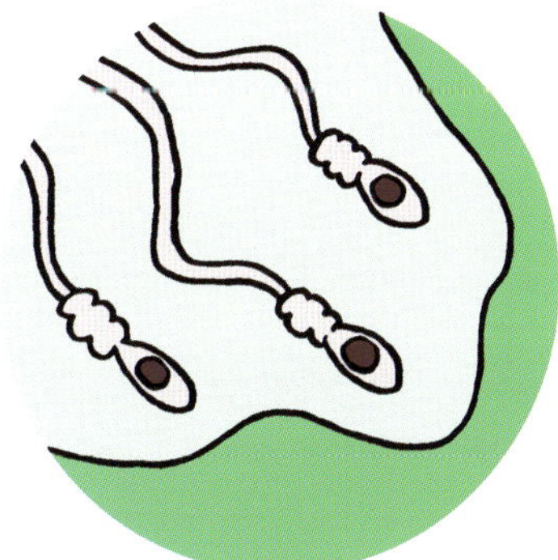

SEMEN

THE FLUID THAT COMES OUT OF THE PENIS DURING EJACULATION. SEMEN CONTAINS SPERM AND FLUIDS FROM THE SEMINAL VESICLE AND PROSTATE GLAND.

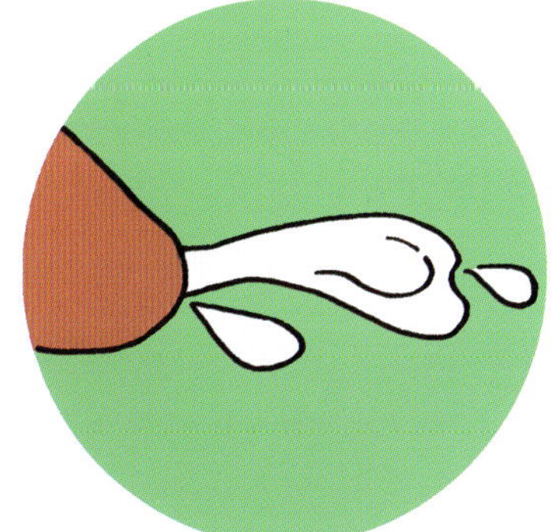

EJACULATION

WHEN SEMEN (ABOUT 1-2 TEASPOONS) EXISTS FROM AN ERECT PENIS. EACH HEALTHY EJACULATION CONTAINS UP TO 200 TO 500 MILLION SPERM!

THE VULVA AND VAGINA

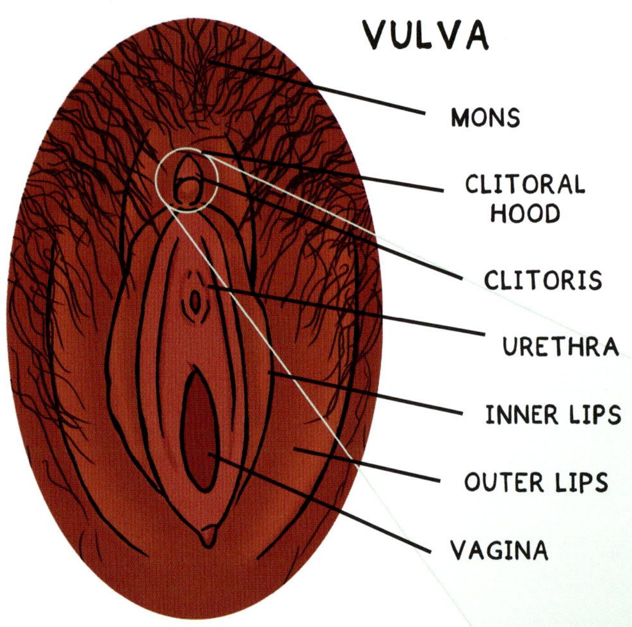

VAGINA - A STRETCHY MUSCULAR PASSAGE THAT CAN BECOME WET WHEN SEXUALLY AROUSED. MENSTRUAL BLOOD WILL EXIT THE BODY HERE.

VULVA - THE EXTERNAL GENITALIA. IT INCLUDES THE MONS, OUTER LIPS, INNER LIPS, CLITORAL HOOD, CLITORIS, URETHRA, AND VAGINA. SOMETIMES PEOPLE INCORRECTLY REFER TO THIS AS THE VAGINA (THE VAGINA IS THE HOLE).

CLITORAL HOOD - A FOLD OF SKIN THAT COVERS AND PROTECTS THE CLITORIS.

CLITORIS - A SENSITIVE GLAND MADE OUT OF ERECTILE TISSUE THAT CAN BECOME ERECT WHEN AROUSED (SEXUALLY EXCITED).

URETHRA - THIS TUBE CONNECTS TO THE BLADDER TO EXPEL URINE FROM THE BODY.

CLITORIS

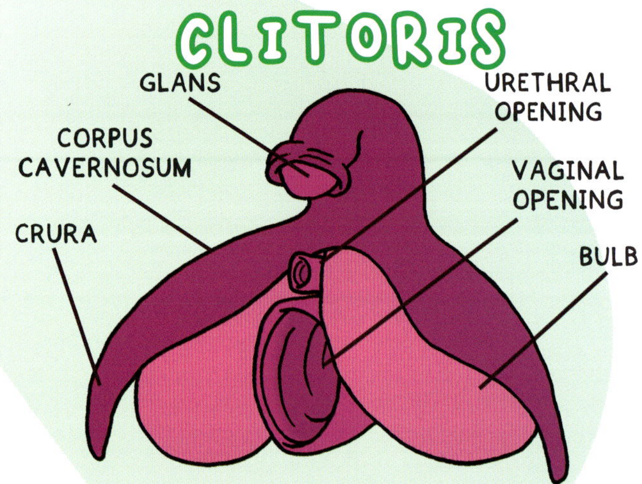

MONS - THIS IS A FATTY SKIN TISSUE THAT PROTECTS THE VULVA. PUBIC HAIR ALSO GROWS ON THE MONS TO HELP PROTECT AGAINST FRICTION.

OUTER LIPS - THESE LIPS HAVE THICKER SKIN TISSUE AND NERVE ENDINGS THAT COVER AND PROTECT THE VULVA.

INNER LIPS - THESE LIPS ARE THINNER AND LINED WITH SENSITIVE NERVE ENDINGS. THESE PROTECT THE OPENINGS TO THE URETHRA AND VAGINA.

SOME CLITERACY

- THE CLITORIS HAS OVER 8,000 NERVE ENDINGS.
- THE CLITORIS IS THE ONLY ORGAN THAT EXISTS EXCLUSIVELY FOR PLEASURE.
- SCIENTISTS DISCOVERED THE WHOLE STRUCTURE OF THE CLITORIS IN 1998.

INVENTIONS BEFORE THE DISCOVERY OF THE CLITORIS:

- **1983** THE INTERNET
- **1994** THE PLAYSTATION
- **1996** SCIENTISTS CLONED A SHEEP NAMED DOLLY!
- **1997** NETFLIX FOUNDED

THE INTERNET

DOLLY THE SHEEP

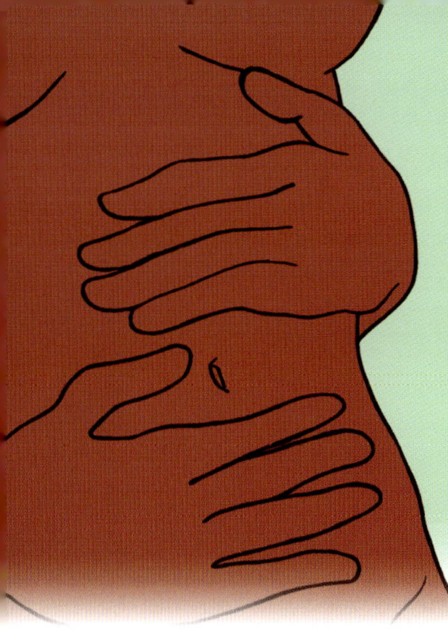

MASTURBATION

MASTURBATION IS WHEN SOMEONE TOUCHES THEIR OWN BODY TO EXPERIENCE PLEASURE.

MASTURBATION GIVES PEOPLE THE OPPORTUNITY TO EXPLORE THEIR BODIES SAFELY.

YOU CAN DETERMINE HOW YOUR BODY RESPONDS TO CERTAIN TOUCHES AND DISCOVER WHAT FEELS GOOD.

SOME PEOPLE *CHOOSE* TO MASTURBATE, AND SOME *DO NOT*.

BOTH ARE NORMAL.

MYTHS	FACTS
MASTURBATING CAN GIVE YOU PIMPLES AND ACNE	MASTURBATING WILL NOT GIVE YOU PIMPLES OR ACNE. THIS MYTH HAS BEEN AROUND SINCE OUR GRANDPARENTS WERE KIDS.
YOU CAN'T MASTURBATE IF YOU'RE IN A RELATIONSHIP	YOU CAN CHOOSE TO MASTURBATE IF YOU ARE IN A RELATIONSHIP. THIS MYTH COMES FROM THE IDEA THAT YOUR PARTNER SHOULD BE THE ONLY ONE EXPLORING YOUR BODY IF YOU ARE IN A RELATIONSHIP.
ONLY GUYS MASTURBATE	ANY PERSON CAN CHOOSE TO MASTURBATE, REGARDLESS OF THEIR GENDER.
YOU ARE NOT A VIRGIN IF YOU MASTURBATE	"VIRGINITY" IS A WORD THAT MEANS SOMETHING DIFFERENT TO EVERYONE. SOME PEOPLE ASSOCIATE THIS WITH HAVING A SEXUAL ENCOUNTER. SOMEONE WHO MASTURBATES SAFELY EXPLORES AND UNDERSTANDS THEIR OWN BODY IN A WAY THAT DOES NOT INVOLVE A PARTNER.
MASTURBATING IS "DIRTY"	SOME PEOPLE ARE EMBARRASSED ABOUT MASTURBATING BECAUSE THERE ARE MESSAGES ABOUT IT BEING "DIRTY" OR "SHAMEFUL." THERE IS NOTHING WRONG WITH MASTURBATION. MASTURBATION IS NORMAL AND HEALTHY. SOME PEOPLE CHOOSE TO MASTURBATE, AND SOME PEOPLE DON'T.
EVENTUALLY, YOU WILL BECOME ADDICTED TO MASTURBATING	IF YOU'RE SKIPPING SCHOOL, IGNORING FRIENDS AND FAMILY, AND LOSING INTEREST IN BINGE-WATCHING YOUR FAVORITE SHOWS JUST TO STAY HOME AND MASTURBATE, YOU MIGHT BE DOING IT TOO OFTEN. HOWEVER, IT'S IMPORTANT TO KNOW THAT MASTURBATING FREQUENTLY DOESN'T AUTOMATICALLY MEAN SOMEONE IS ADDICTED.

SEXUAL PLEASURE

IN ADDITION TO THE **GENITALS**, THERE ARE OTHER BODY PARTS WHERE SOMEONE CAN EXPERIENCE PLEASURE.

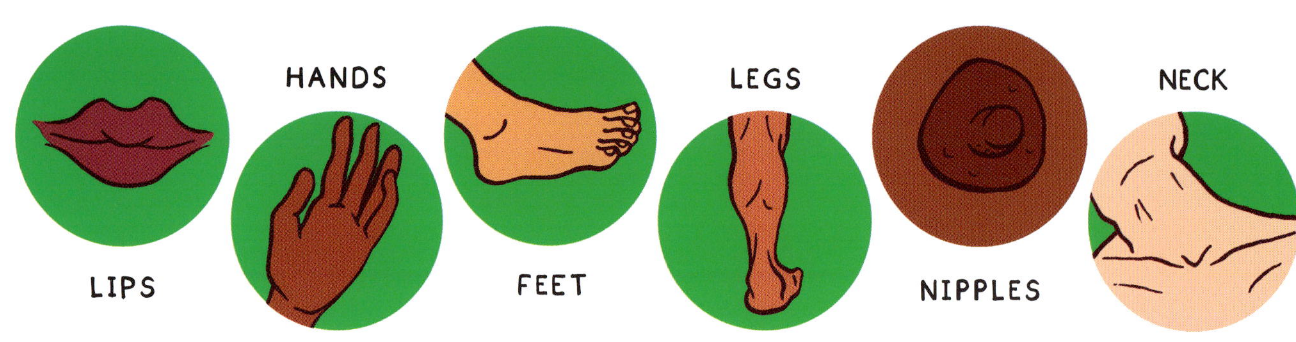

EVERYONE'S BODY IS DIFFERENT IN WHAT THEY FIND PLEASURABLE!

SEXUAL RESPONSE CYCLE

IN MOST PORN, PLEASURE USUALLY FOCUSES ON THE GENITALS AND **DOES NOT SHOW** OTHER BODY PARTS THAT CAN EXPERIENCE PLEASURE.

WHEN SOMEONE IS FEELING SEXUALLY EXCITED OR ENGAGING IN MASTURBATION, OUR BODIES GO THROUGH SOME PHYSICAL STAGES.

THESE STAGES ARE KNOWN AS THE SEXUAL RESPONSE CYCLE.

THE SEXUAL RESPONSE CYCLE IS MADE UP OF 5 STAGES:

I LIKE TO COMPARE THESE STAGES TO RIDING A ROLLERCOASTER!

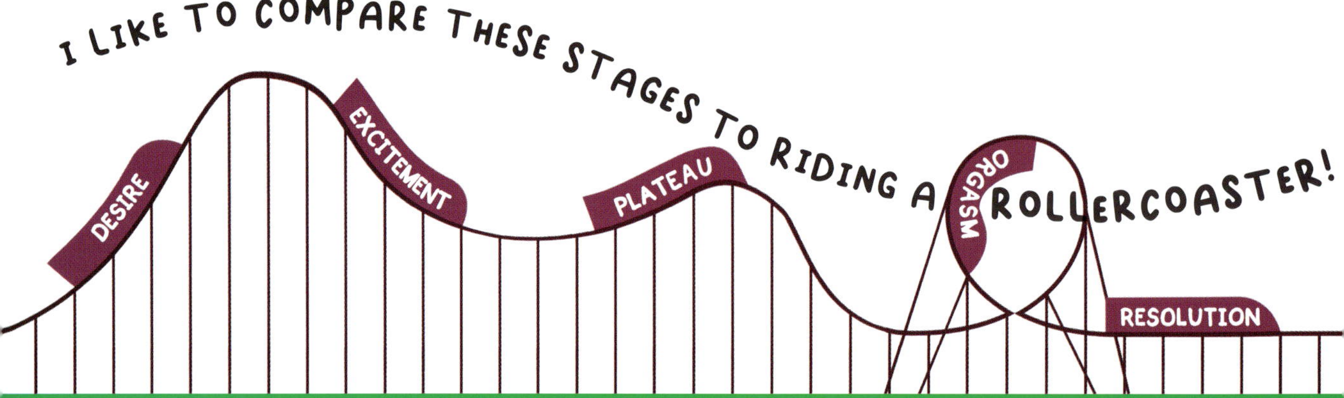

THESE ARE STAGES THAT SOME PEOPLE CAN PHYSICALLY EXPERIENCE. OUR THOUGHTS AND EMOTIONS ALSO INFLUENCE THEM.

DESIRE

THINKING OF BEING SEXUALLY EXCITED. SOMEONE HAS THE DESIRE TO HAVE AN ORGASM OR TO WANT TO HAVE SEX. PEOPLE CAN HAVE DESIRES AND NOT ACT ON THEIR FEELINGS.

SOMEONE HAS THE DESIRE TO WANT TO RIDE THAT ROLLERCOASTER. ARE YOU WILLING TO WAIT THAT LONG FOR THE RIDE?

EXCITEMENT

FEELING HORNY. IT IS WHEN SOMEONE'S BODY MAY PHYSICALLY RESPOND TO THEIR THOUGHTS OF DESIRE. SOME BODILY RESPONSES CAN INCLUDE: HAVING AN ERECTION, THE VAGINA MAY LUBRICATE, OR THE PALMS OF THE HANDS MIGHT BE SWEATY.

YOU'RE STANDING IN LINE, KNOWING THAT YOU'RE NEXT TO GO ON THE RIDE. YOU MIGHT FEEL THE SENSATION OF BUTTERFLIES IN YOUR STOMACH, AND YOUR PALMS MIGHT BE SWEATY!

PLATEAU

THE BODY IS EXPERIENCING BLOOD RUSHING TO THE GENITALS. SOMEONE'S HEART RATE WILL BEGIN TO INCREASE WITH THE SENSATION OF PLEASURE IN THEIR GENITALS. THIS FEELING IS BECOMING INTENSIFIED.

THE RIDE HAS STARTED, AND THE TRACK IS SLOWLY REACHING THE TOP. YOUR EXCITEMENT INTENSIFIES BECAUSE THAT RIDE WILL DROP AND GO FAST ONCE YOU REACH THE TOP!

ORGASM

THE REPRODUCTIVE ORGANS AND GENITALS BEGIN TO CONTRACT. MOST PENISES EJACULATE DURING THIS STAGE. THE CLITORIS AND VAGINA EXPERIENCE PLEASURABLE SENSATIONS AND A FEELING OF "RELEASE."

THE RIDE IS HAPPENING! THERE ARE LOOPS, IT'S GOING FAST, YOUR HEART RATE IS HIGH. THIS RIDE IS EVERYTHING!

RESOLUTION

THE BODY RETURNS TO A REGULAR RESTING HEART RATE, ERECT OR SWOLLEN BODY PARTS RETURN TO NORMAL, AND SKIN FLUSHING DISAPPEARS. SOME PEOPLE MIGHT EXPERIENCE A FEELING OF CALMNESS.

THE RIDE IS OVER AND SLOWING DOWN. YOUR HEART RATE AND BODY RETURN TO NORMAL. THE WAIT FOR THE RIDE WAS WORTH IT!

A FRIENDLY REMINDER THAT...

ALL GENITALS ARE NORMAL!

ANATOMY CROSSWORD

FILL OUT THE CROSSWORD PUZZLE WITH THE CORRECT TERMS USING THE GIVEN CLUES.

DOWN:

1. A GLAND WITH MORE THAN 8,000 NERVE ENDINGS, AND ITS SOLE PURPOSE IS EXPERIENCING PLEASURE.
2. THE TUBE WHERE URINE EXITS THE BODY.
4. DURING THE STAGES OF SEXUAL PLEASURE, THIS STAGE INVOLVES REPRODUCTIVE ORGANS AND GENITALS CONTRACTING.
6. WHEN SEMEN (ABOUT 1-2 TEASPOONS) COMES OUT OF AN ERECT PENIS.
7. LINED WITH PLEASURE-SENSITIVE NERVE ENDINGS AND IS MADE OF SPONGY TISSUE THAT FILLS UP WITH BLOOD WHEN AROUSED (SEXUALLY EXCITED).
9. THE FLUID THAT COMES OUT OF THE PENIS DURING EJACULATION.

ACROSS:

3. ALL EXTERNAL GENITALS COMBINED, INCLUDING THE URETHRA, VAGINA, INNER LIPS, OUTER LIPS, AND MONS.
4. DURING THE STAGES OF SEXUAL PLEASURE, THIS STAGE INCLUDES THINKING ABOUT BEING SEXUALLY EXCITED.
8. WHEN SOMEONE EXPLORES THEIR OWN BODY TO EXPERIENCE PLEASURE.
10. A REPRODUCTIVE CELL; LOOKS LIKE A TADPOLE UNDER A MICROSCOPE.
11. THE REPRODUCTIVE ORGANS LOCATED ON THE OUTSIDE OF THE BODY.
12. LAYER OF SKIN THAT COVERS AND PROTECTS THE GLANS OF THE PENIS.
13. WHERE MENSTRUAL BLOOD EXITS THE BODY.

*ANSWERS IN BACK OF BOOK

5

CONSENT AND COMMUNICATION

THIS CHAPTER DISCUSSES THE DIFFERENCE BETWEEN COMMUNICATION IN PORNOGRAPHY AND COMMUNICATION IN REAL LIFE.

ONCE YOU COMPLETE THIS CHAPTER, FIND YOUR TRUSTED ADULT TO TALK TO AND ASK ANY QUESTIONS YOU HAVE.

IN MOST PORN, THE PERFORMERS NEGOTIATE THEIR BOUNDARIES BEFORE A SCENE BEGINS.

WHEN THIS HAPPENS, EACH PERSON COMMUNICATES WHAT THEY ARE COMFORTABLE DOING.

BOUNDARIES

RULES OR LIMITS A PERSON CREATES TO IDENTIFY SAFE WAYS FOR OTHERS TO BEHAVE TOWARDS THEM AND HOW THEY WILL RESPOND WHEN SOMEONE CROSSES THEIR LIMITS.

PEOPLE USE WORDS THAT THEY MAY NOT TYPICALLY SAY DURING SEX LIKE

SAFE WORDS LET OTHERS KNOW THAT SOMEBODY CROSSED YOUR BOUNDARIES OR THAT YOU NEED A BREAK.

IN PORN, IT IS NOT COMMON TO SEE THIS TYPE OF COMMUNICATION.

ONE REASON IS THAT SOME DIRECTORS FIND IT BORING AND DON'T WANT TO FILM IT.

IT IS WHY MOST PORN SHOWS PEOPLE HAVING SEX RIGHT AWAY.

THAT'S IT! WE DON'T SEE ANYTHING ELSE.

THE ONLY WAY SOMEONE WILL KNOW WHAT THEY WANT DURING A SEXUAL EXPERIENCE IS WHEN YOU TALK TO THEM ABOUT IT.

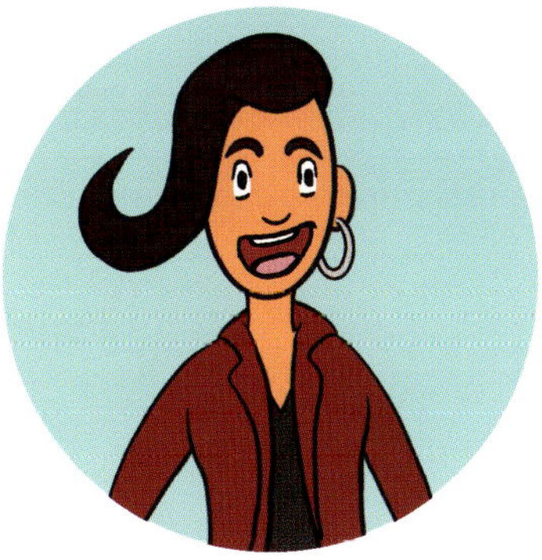

NO ONE IS A MIND READER.

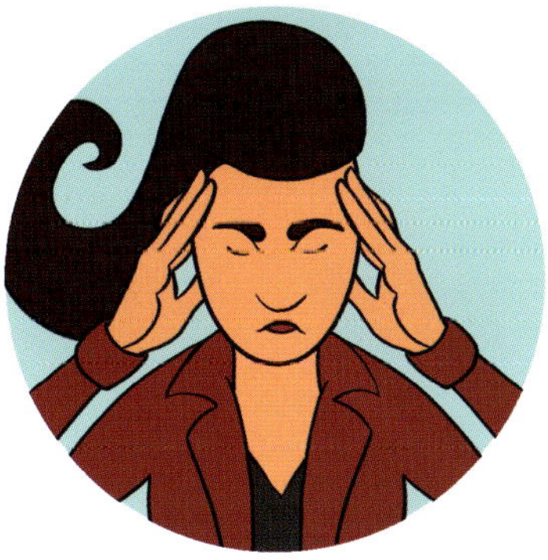

WE DON'T GROW UP ALREADY KNOWING EVERYTHING ABOUT SEX AND PLEASURE.

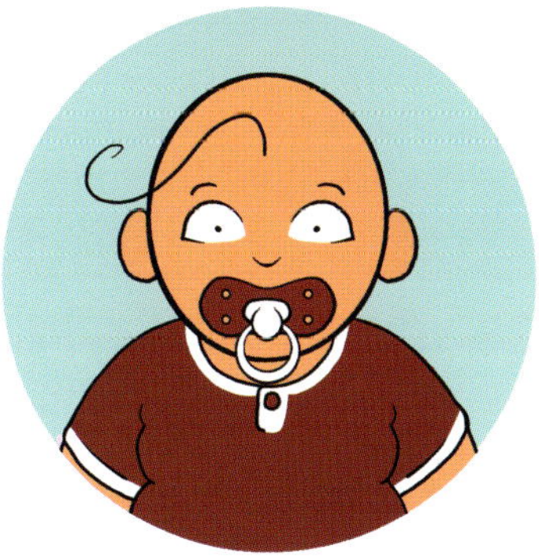

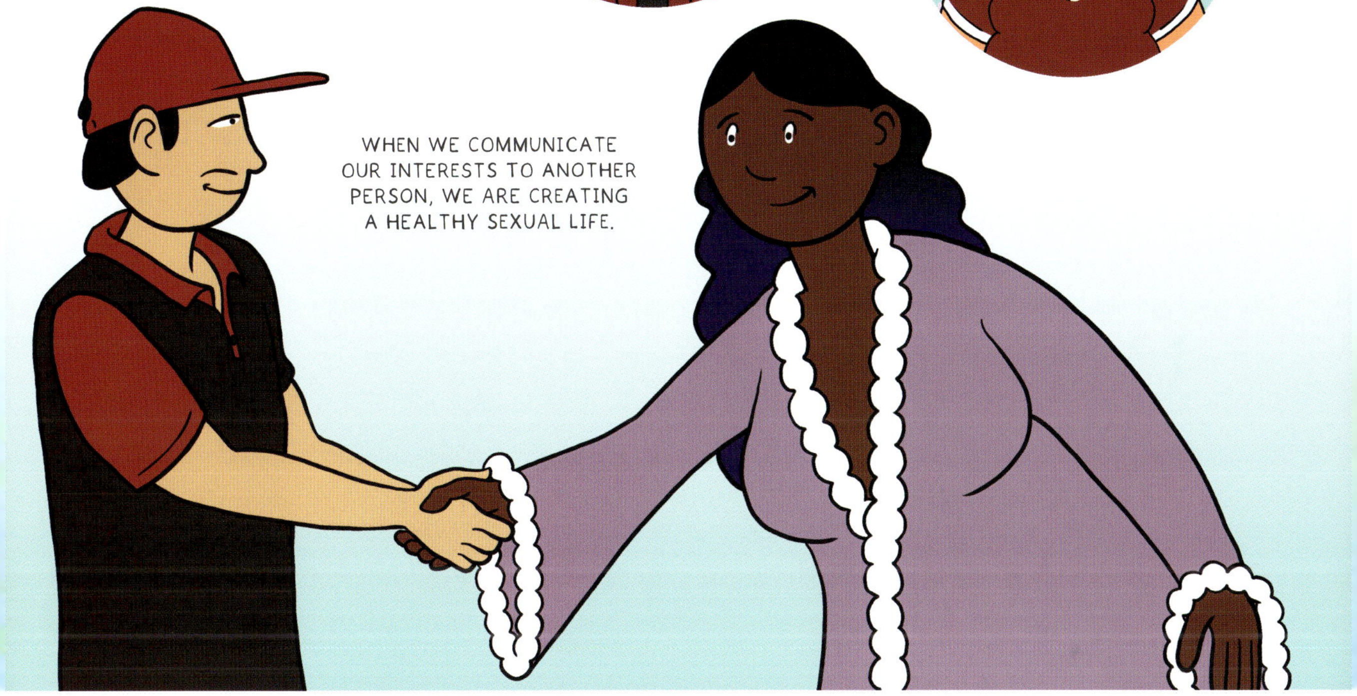

WHEN WE COMMUNICATE OUR INTERESTS TO ANOTHER PERSON, WE ARE CREATING A HEALTHY SEXUAL LIFE.

PORN SHOWS LOTS OF PENISES, VULVAS, AND ORGASMS, BUT IT DOESN'T ALWAYS SHOW THE THINGS ABOUT SEX THAT MOST PEOPLE VALUE:

ASK YOUR ADULT

WHEN YOU WERE MY AGE, DID YOU EVER FACE ANY CHALLENGES WITH COMMUNICATION?

HOW DID YOU GET OVER IT?

HOW CAN I GET BETTER AT TALKING TO PEOPLE AND SAYING WHAT I WANT WITH CONFIDENCE?

YOU MIGHT BE CONSENTING TO...

A HUG

A HANDSHAKE

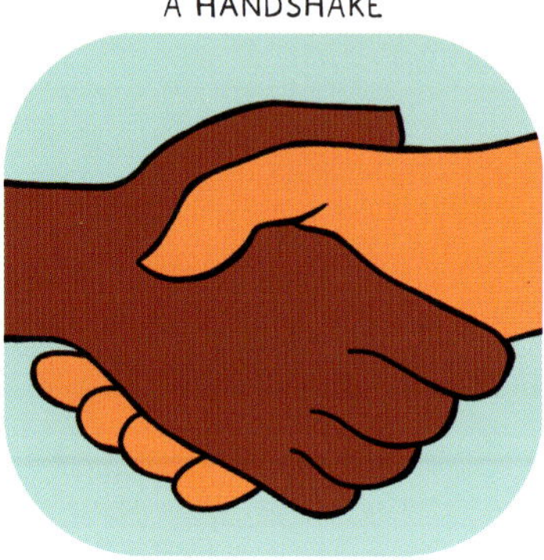

HAVING A CHAT WITH SOMEONE

CONSENT APPLIES TO **EVERYONE** REGARDLESS OF GENDER, AGE, OR SEXUAL ORIENTATION

WHEN TALKING ABOUT CONSENT AND SEX, A LOT MORE GOES INTO SOMEONE SAYING YES OR NO.

CONSENT MUST BE SOBER.

WHEN WE PUT SUBSTANCES INTO OUR BODIES, OUR DECISION-MAKING PROCESS CHANGES. IT'S IMPORTANT TO UNDERSTAND HOW DRUGS AND ALCOHOL PLAY A ROLE IN YOUR LIFE.

WHEN SOMEONE IS UNDER THE INFLUENCE, THEY ***CANNOT*** LEGALLY CONSENT TO SEX.

CONSENT MUST BE AUTHENTIC.

TO BE AUTHENTIC MEANS BEING TRUE TO YOUR YES. THINK ABOUT A TIME WHEN YOU HEARD A YES THAT SOUNDED LIKE A NO.

WHAT DID THAT SOUND LIKE?

SOUND FAMILIAR? THESE ARE NOT AUTHENTIC ANSWERS. IT'S ALSO IMPORTANT TO ASK YOURSELF:

DO I FEEL **SAFE** SAYING NO?
DO I FEEL COMFORTABLE TELLING SOMEONE **I'M NOT READY**?

CONSENT MUST BE ENTHUSIASTIC.

DO YOU GENUINELY WANT TO ENGAGE IN THIS, OR ARE YOU DOING IT BECAUSE SOMEONE ELSE WANTS TO?

BEING ENTHUSIASTIC MEANS THAT YOU ARE CONFIDENT WITH YOUR YES.

THINK ABOUT A TIME YOU WERE AT HOME WATCHING TV OR PLAYING VIDEO GAMES.

ONE OF YOUR ADULTS WALKS INTO YOUR ROOM TO ASK YOU TO GO CLEAN THE DISHES.

YOU KNOW YOU WOULD RATHER BE DOING ANYTHING BUT THE DISHES RIGHT NOW.

HOWEVER, YOU KNOW THIS IS ONE OF YOUR CHORES SO YOU ANSWER,

YOU DID NOT WANT TO CLEAN THE DISHES, BUT YOU DID THEM ANYWAY BECAUSE YOUR ADULT "SUGGESTED" IT TO YOU.

THIS IS NOT AN EXAMPLE OF AUTHENTIC CONSENT.

NOW IMAGINE BEING OUT OF SCHOOL AND HANGING OUT WITH YOUR BEST FRIEND.

AT ONE POINT, YOUR FRIEND TELLS YOU,

FOR MOST OF US, WE WOULD BE CONSENTING TO FREE LUNCH.

THIS IS AN EXAMPLE OF AUTHENTIC CONSENT. SEE THE DIFFERENCE?

YOU ARE BEING TRUE TO YOUR YES.

THE MORE YOU CAN PRACTICE AND UNDERSTAND WHAT IT MEANS TO BE AUTHENTIC, THE BETTER YOU WILL BE ABLE TO WORK THROUGH THIS PROCESS.

WE ALL HAVE TO START SOMEWHERE.

TRY IT OUT FOR YOURSELF IN THESE NEXT ACTIVITIES.

WAYS TO ASK FOR CONSENT

WHEN CONSIDERING BEING INTIMATE (LIKE HAVING SEX) WITH A PARTNER, THERE ARE SEVERAL WAYS TO ASK FOR CONSENT. IT'S ALSO IMPORTANT TO KNOW THAT CONSENT IS CONSTANT DURING INTIMACY, MEANING IT WILL ALWAYS OCCUR. FOR EXAMPLE, CONSENT WILL OCCUR AT THE BEGINNING OF INTIMACY, DURING, AND AFTER.

HERE ARE SOME EXAMPLES OF HOW TO PRACTICE ASKING FOR CONSENT WITH A PARTNER. FILL IN YOUR OWN WAYS TO ASK FOR CONSENT IN THE BLANKS!

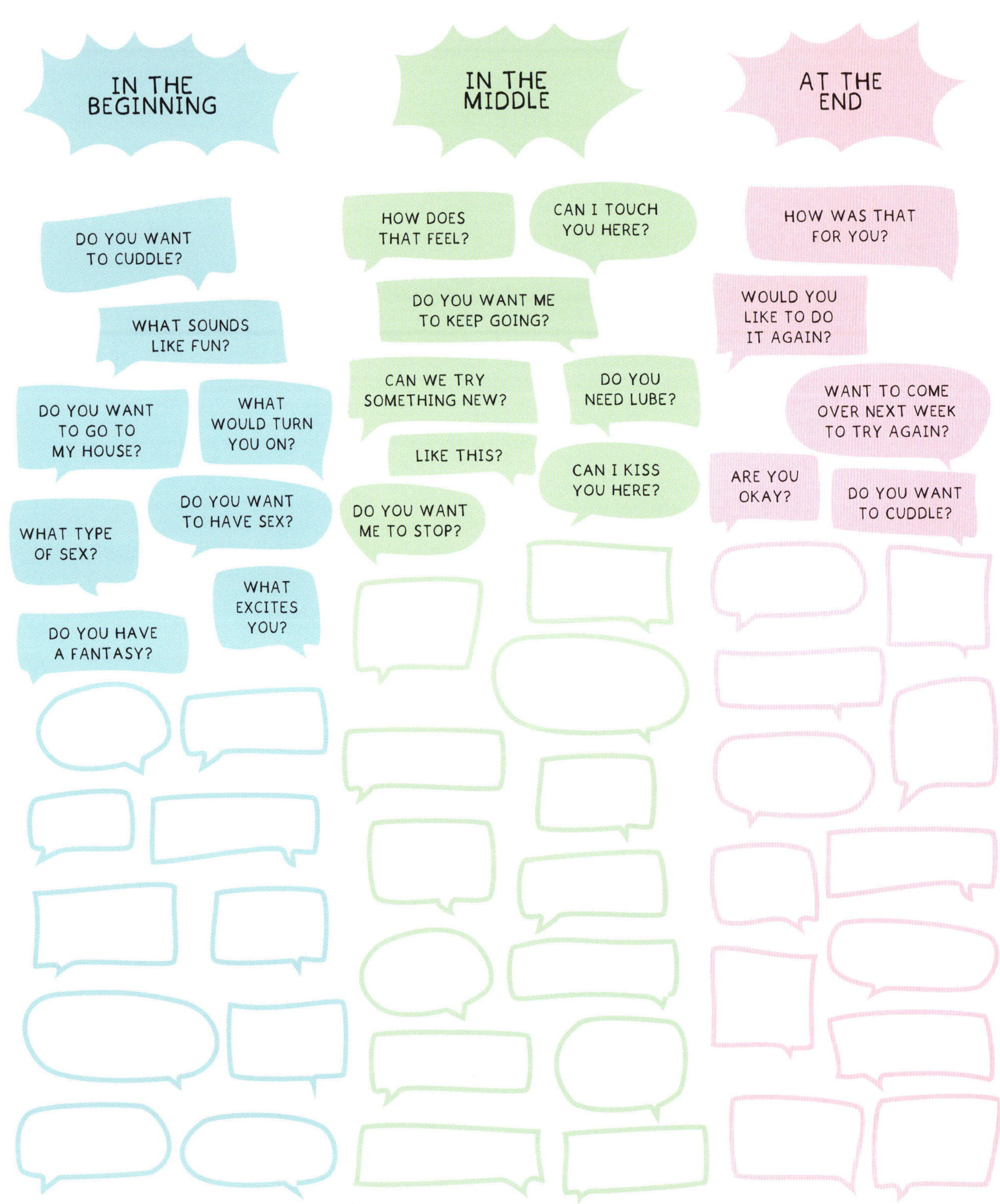

REMINDER: CONSENT IS REVERSIBLE AND CAN BE TAKEN BACK AT ANY TIME.

FORCING PEOPLE INTO DOING SOMETHING IS NOT CONSENT.

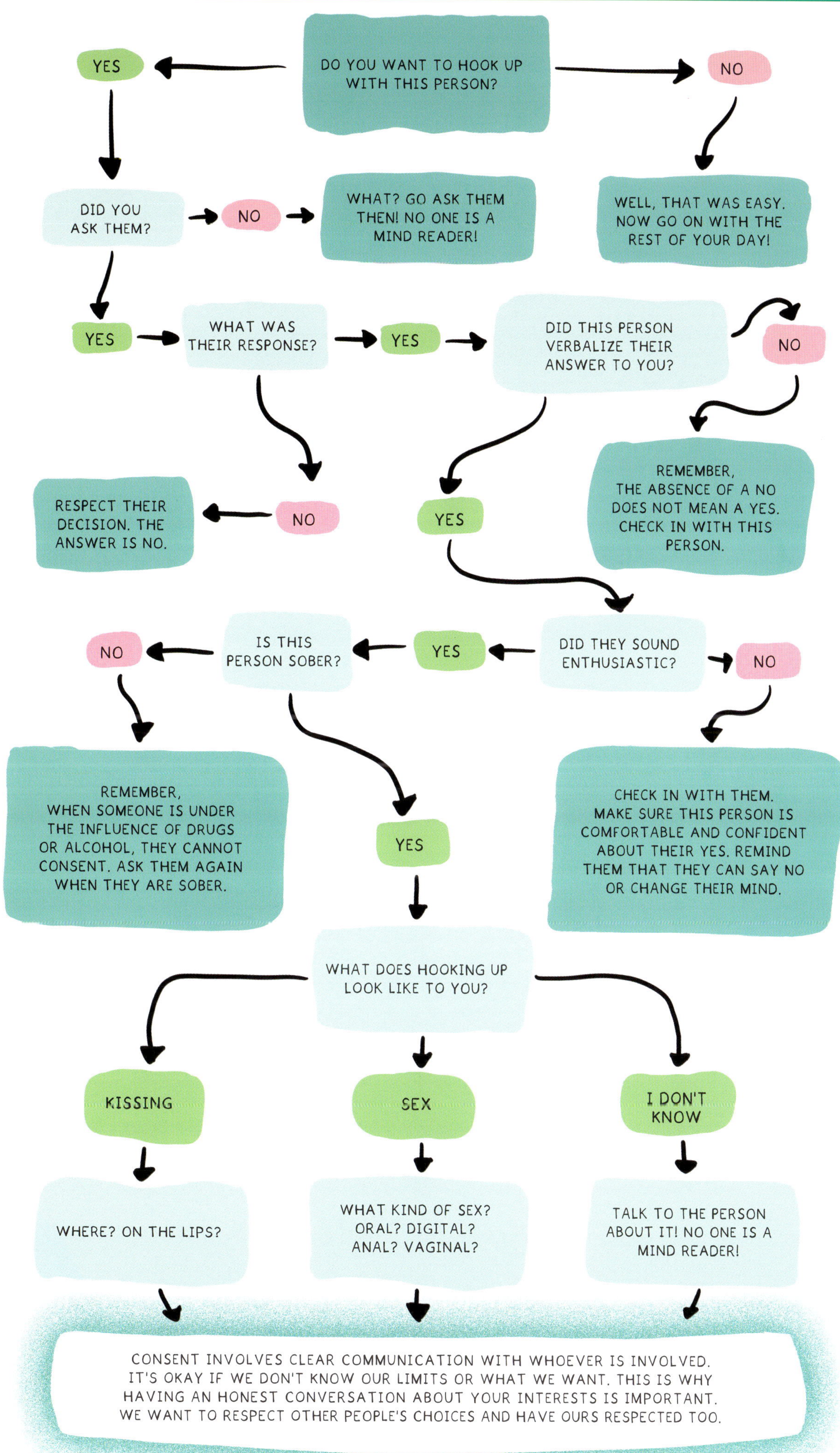
DO YOU WANT TO HOOK UP WITH THIS PERSON?
YES
NO
WELL, THAT WAS EASY. NOW GO ON WITH THE REST OF YOUR DAY!
DID YOU ASK THEM?
NO
WHAT? GO ASK THEM THEN! NO ONE IS A MIND READER!
YES
WHAT WAS THEIR RESPONSE?
YES
DID THIS PERSON VERBALIZE THEIR ANSWER TO YOU?
NO
REMEMBER, THE ABSENCE OF A NO DOES NOT MEAN A YES. CHECK IN WITH THIS PERSON.
NO
RESPECT THEIR DECISION. THE ANSWER IS NO.
YES
DID THEY SOUND ENTHUSIASTIC?
NO
CHECK IN WITH THEM. MAKE SURE THIS PERSON IS COMFORTABLE AND CONFIDENT ABOUT THEIR YES. REMIND THEM THAT THEY CAN SAY NO OR CHANGE THEIR MIND.
YES
IS THIS PERSON SOBER?
NO
REMEMBER, WHEN SOMEONE IS UNDER THE INFLUENCE OF DRUGS OR ALCOHOL, THEY CANNOT CONSENT. ASK THEM AGAIN WHEN THEY ARE SOBER.
YES
WHAT DOES HOOKING UP LOOK LIKE TO YOU?
KISSING
SEX
I DON'T KNOW
WHERE? ON THE LIPS?
WHAT KIND OF SEX? ORAL? DIGITAL? ANAL? VAGINAL?
TALK TO THE PERSON ABOUT IT! NO ONE IS A MIND READER!
CONSENT INVOLVES CLEAR COMMUNICATION WITH WHOEVER IS INVOLVED. IT'S OKAY IF WE DON'T KNOW OUR LIMITS OR WHAT WE WANT. THIS IS WHY HAVING AN HONEST CONVERSATION ABOUT YOUR INTERESTS IS IMPORTANT. WE WANT TO RESPECT OTHER PEOPLE'S CHOICES AND HAVE OURS RESPECTED TOO.

6

THIS CHAPTER WILL DISCUSS IDEAS OF HOW SOME PEOPLE DEFINE THE WORD "SEX." IT WILL ALSO DISCUSS THE TYPE OF SEXUAL HEALTH EDUCATION PEOPLE MIGHT RECEIVE IN SCHOOL.

ONCE YOU COMPLETE THIS CHAPTER, FIND YOUR TRUSTED ADULT TO TALK TO AND ASK ANY QUESTIONS YOU HAVE.

PORN IS **FICTION**

PORN IS A **FANTASY**

PORN IS

- BEAUTY IDEALS
- COMMUNICATION
- CONSENT
- OTHER UNREALISTIC EXPECTATIONS

HOWEVER, IT IS **NORMAL** TO BE CURIOUS AND HAVE QUESTIONS ABOUT SEX.

WHAT IS SEX ANYWAY?

EVERYONE HAS A DIFFERENT IDEA OF WHAT IS CONSIDERED SEX. SOME CAN INCLUDE:

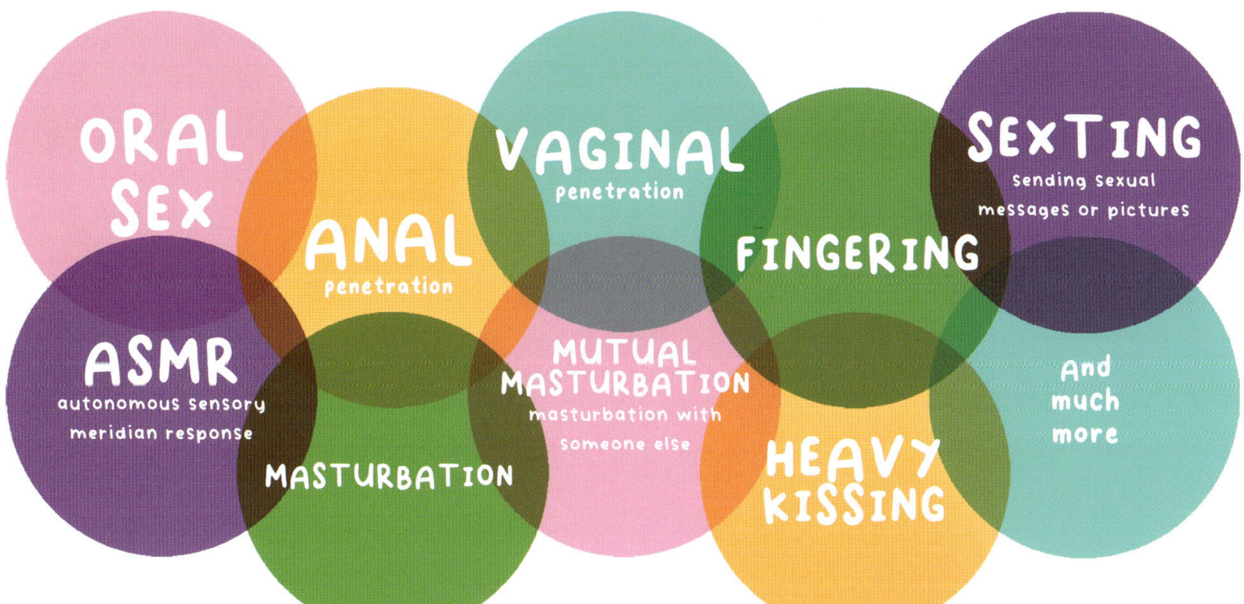

HERE ARE A FEW QUESTIONS TO ASK YOURSELF:		
AM I FEELING PRESSURE FROM OTHERS TO HAVE SEX?	YES	NO
DO I KNOW WHY I WANT TO HAVE SEX?	YES	NO
CAN I COMFORTABLY TALK TO MY PARTNER ABOUT SEX?	YES	NO
DO I FEEL SAFE COMMUNICATING MY BOUNDARIES?	YES	NO
DO I HAVE SOMEONE I CAN SAFELY TALK TO ABOUT MY DECISION TO HAVE SEX?	YES	NO

Sex Education in Schools

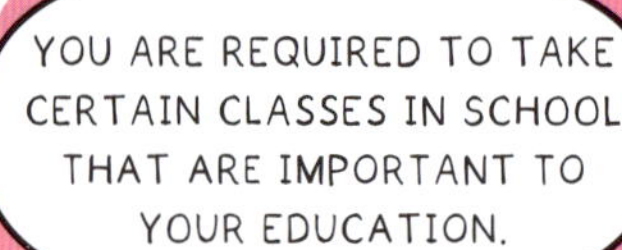

IN MANY SCHOOLS, SEX EDUCATION IS *NOT* A REQUIREMENT.

FOR INSTANCE, IN CALIFORNIA, ALL PUBLIC AND CHARTER SCHOOLS, BOTH MIDDLE AND HIGH SCHOOLS, MUST TEACH COMPREHENSIVE SEX EDUCATION.

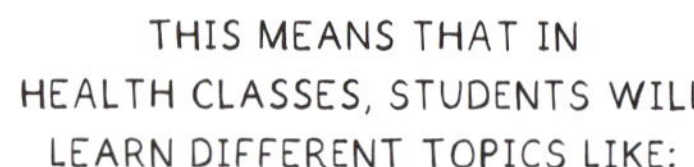

ABSTINENCE

BIRTH CONTROL

SEXUAL ORIENTATION

CONDOMS

GENDER

HEALTHY RELATIONSHIPS

CONSENT

AND MUCH MORE...

THE GOAL IS TO APPLY THAT INFORMATION TO A PERSON'S LIFE TO HELP MAKE DECISIONS ABOUT THEIR HEALTH.

SEX EDUCATION IS NOT ABOUT WHAT YOU *SHOULD* OR *SHOULD NOT* DO.

IT'S ABOUT GIVING YOU INFORMATION SO YOU CAN FEEL EMPOWERED TO MAKE THE DECISION FOR YOURSELF.

UNFORTUNATELY, NOT ALL SCHOOLS IN THE **UNITED STATES** REQUIRE SEX EDUCATION.

SOME STATES ONLY FOCUS ON ABSTINENCE-ONLY EDUCATION.

ABSTINENCE-ONLY MEANS TEACHING STUDENTS THAT THEIR ONLY CHOICE IS TO ABSTAIN FROM SEXUAL ENCOUNTERS.

BACK-TO-SCHOOL STATISTICS

AS OF 2024 IN THE U.S., JUST 37 STATES AND DC REQUIRE SEX AND HIV EDUCATION IN SCHOOLS.

ALSO, IN THE U.S., 33 STATES EMPHASIZE ABSTINENCE EDUCATION.

OF THOSE, 26 STATES AND DC REQUIRE THAT THE INFORMATION BE MEDICALLY ACCURATE.

ONLY 11 STATES AND DC REQUIRE THE IMPORTANCE OF CONSENT TO SEXUAL ACTIVITY TO BE COVERED.

TAKE A LOOK AT THE MAPS BELOW.

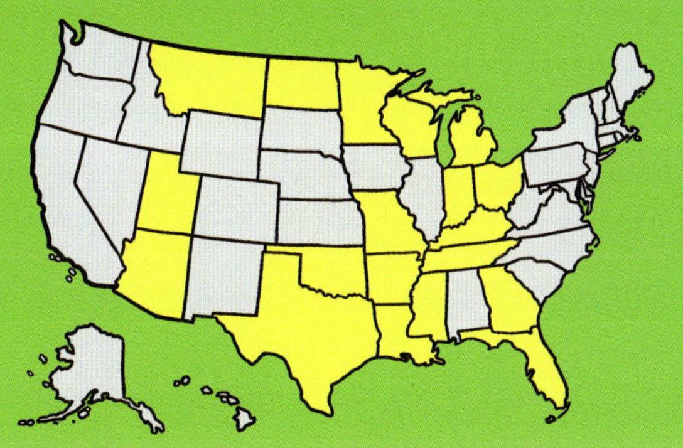

ABSTINENCE-ONLY EDUCATION

SOURCE: *GUTTMACHER INSTITUTE, 2023*

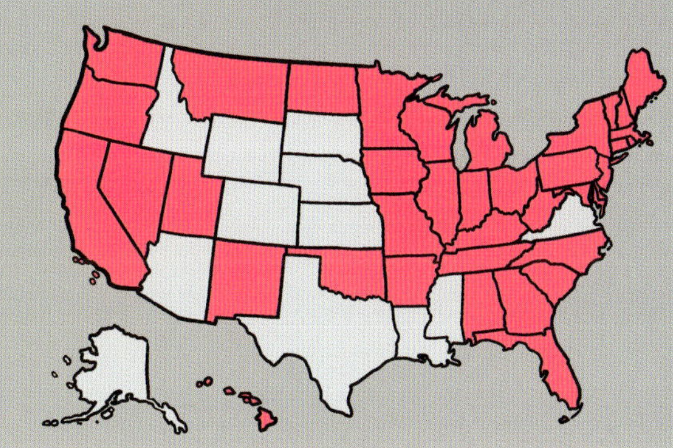

SEX AND HIV EDUCATION

SOURCE: *GUTTMACHER INSTITUTE, 2023*

YOU MIGHT NOTICE ON THE MAPS THAT SOME STATES ARE HIGHLIGHTED TWICE. EVEN THOUGH THEY MAKE SEX AND HIV EDUCATION MANDATORY, SOME OF THOSE STATES MAINLY TEACH ABSTINENCE ONLY.

THAT SOUNDS UNFAIR!

SO ONLY SOME STATES TEACH SEX ED?

WHY?

YOU'RE RIGHT. IT IS UNFAIR.

SOME ADULTS BELIEVE TEACHING SEX EDUCATION IN SCHOOLS WILL ENCOURAGE ALL YOUNG PEOPLE TO ENGAGE IN SEXUAL ACTIVITY. THESE ARE THE SAME PEOPLE WHO CREATE THESE LAWS.

WOW! JUST BECAUSE I'M TRYING TO UNDERSTAND HOW MY BODY WORKS DOESN'T MEAN I'M GOING TO GO OUT AND DO IT!

THIS IS A BIG REASON WHY PEOPLE WATCH PORN TO UNDERSTAND BODIES AND SEX.

BECAUSE SOME PEOPLE CANNOT LEARN ABOUT IT IN SCHOOL, THEY WILL TURN TO PORN TO LEARN ABOUT THEIR BODIES AND SEX - WHICH IS PROBLEMATIC.

COMPREHENSIVE SEX EDUCATION IS SO MUCH MORE THAN SEX!

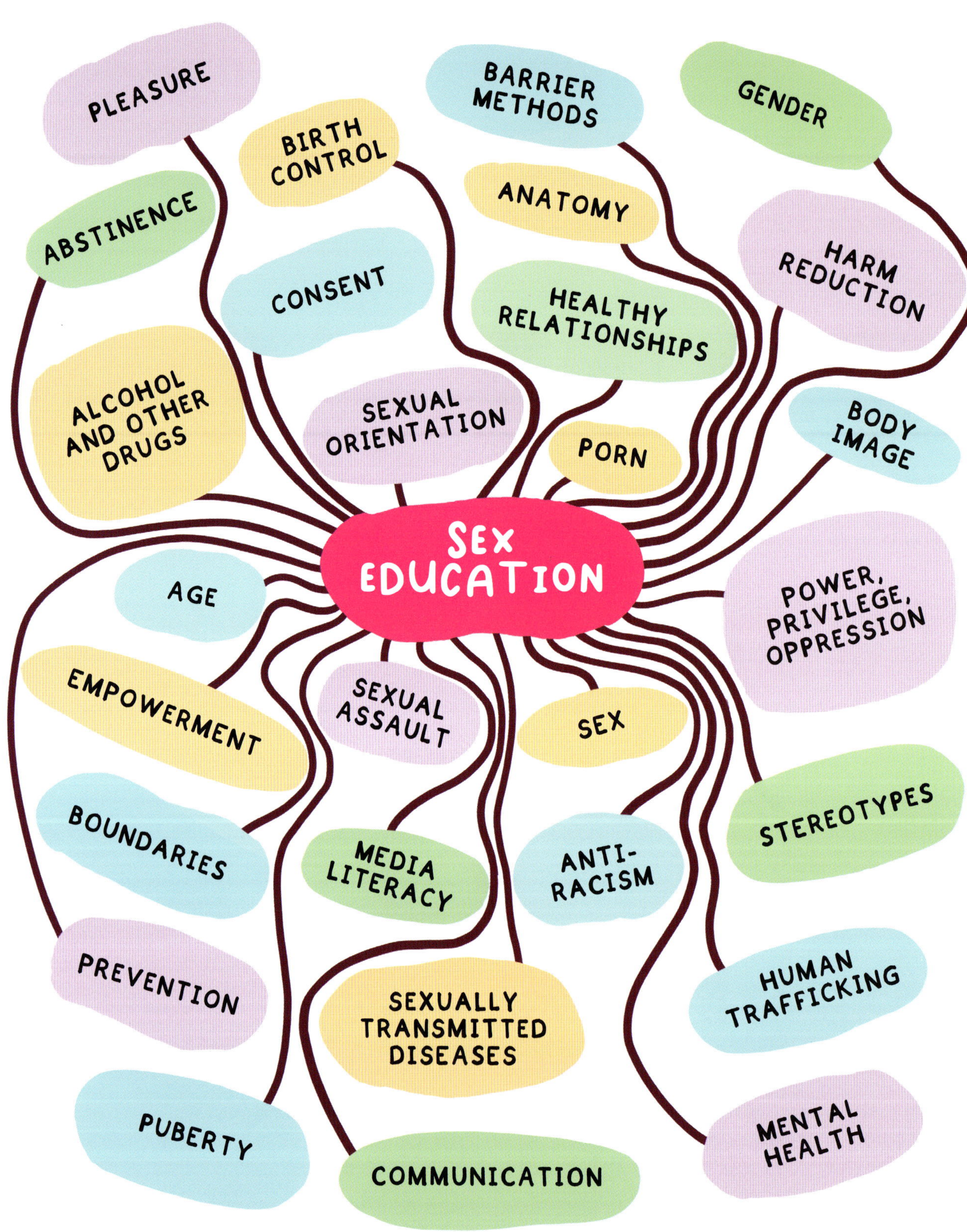

IT INCLUDES ALL THESE DIFFERENT TOPICS AND HOW IT RELATES TO THE PARTS OF YOUR IDVENTITY.

REFLECTION QUESTIONS

ANSWER THE FOLLOWING REFLECTION QUESTIONS TO EXPLORE YOUR THOUGHTS AND FEELINGS ABOUT SEX EDUCATION. INCLUDE A DISCUSSION WITH YOUR TRUSTED ADULT TO GAIN INSIGHT INTO THEIR EDUCATIONAL EXPERIENCE.

ASK YOUR ADULT

WHERE DID YOU LEARN ABOUT SEX EDUCATION?

WHAT WAS THAT EXPERIENCE LIKE FOR YOU?

WAS THERE SOMETHING YOU WANTED TO LEARN MORE ABOUT?

PORNOGRAPHY IS FICTION AND IS NOT A REALISTIC EXAMPLE OF SEX. WHAT TYPE OF IMPACT CAN THIS HAVE ON SOMEONE WHO IS WATCHING PORN TO LEARN ABOUT SEX?

DO YOU THINK ABSTINENCE-ONLY EDUCATION IN SCHOOL WILL POSITIVELY OR NEGATIVELY AFFECT A STUDENT? EXPLAIN.

WHAT IS A TOPIC SURROUNDING SEX AND SEXUALITY YOU WOULD LIKE TO LEARN MORE ABOUT? EXPLAIN.

7

SAFER SEX

THIS CHAPTER DISCUSSES HOW TO KEEP OUR BODIES AND MINDS SAFE DURING SEXUAL ACTIVITY. THERE WILL BE ILLUSTRATIONS OF GENITALS AND HOW TO USE BARRIER METHODS, FOR EDUCATIONAL PURPOSES ONLY.

ONCE YOU COMPLETE THIS CHAPTER, FIND YOUR TRUSTED ADULT TO TALK TO AND ASK ANY QUESTIONS YOU HAVE.

WHAT DOES IT MEAN TO HAVE SAFER SEX?

SAFER SEX MEANS USING TOOLS TO INCREASE HEALTHY RELATIONSHIPS AND PREVENT SEXUALLY TRANSMITTED INFECTIONS (STI'S) AND UNWANTED PREGNANCIES.

THIS INCLUDES USING CONDOMS AND LUBE, DISCUSSING YOUR STI STATUS, TAKING BIRTH CONTROL, AND COMMUNICATING WITH A PARTNER.

ALL OF THIS IS HAVING SAFER SEX.

SEXUALLY TRANSMITTED INFECTION

INFECTION A PERSON CAN GET BY HAVING SEX WITH SOMEONE WHO HAS AN INFECTION.

WHAT DOES SAFER SEX MEAN TO YOU? WRITE YOUR ANSWER BELOW.

____

____

____

____

WHAT DOES SAFER SEX HAVE TO DO WITH PORN?

DURING SCENES IN MOST PORN,

WE DON'T SEE ANYTHING ABOUT SAFER SEX PRACTICES, SIMILAR TO PEOPLE NOT HAVING CONVERSATIONS ABOUT CONSENT.

IT'S RARE IF WE SEE SOMEONE ASKING:

ONCE AGAIN, THIS IS BECAUSE, BEHIND THE SCENES, THE PERFORMERS WILL DISCUSS SAFER SEX OPTIONS.

FOR EXAMPLE, PERFORMERS WILL DECIDE IF THEY WILL USE CONDOMS. A PERFORMER WITH A LATEX ALLERGY MUST COMMUNICATE WHAT NON-LATEX CONDOMS TO USE.

SEXUALLY TRANSMITTED INFECTION (STI) STATUS

ONE OF THE MOST COMMON SYMPTOMS OF HAVING AN STI IS NO SYMPTOMS.

THAT IS WHY IT'S CRUCIAL FOR PEOPLE WHO ARE SEXUALLY ACTIVE TO GET TESTED AT A HEALTH CLINIC REGULARLY.

SYMPTOM

PHYSICAL SIGNS THAT MIGHT INDICATE AN INFECTION

MOST PORN PERFORMERS HAVE TO SIGN A CONTRACT WITH THE COMPANY THEY WORK FOR TO GO THROUGH ROUTINE STI TESTING.

IT IS ALSO ANOTHER REASON WHY SOME PERFORMERS MAY CHOOSE TO USE CONDOMS OR NOT.

EITHER WAY, PORN PERFORMERS PRACTICE SAFER SEX BY GETTING TESTED AND COMMUNICATING THEIR STATUS.

COMMON QUESTIONS ABOUT STI TESTING

CAN YOU GET TESTED PRIVATELY?

YES! TALK TO YOUR DOCTOR AND ASK THEM TO KEEP THE CONVERSATION PRIVATE. IN MANY STATES, ONCE YOU'RE 13, YOU CAN GET TESTED AND TREATED FOR SEXUALLY TRANSMITTED INFECTIONS WITHOUT NEEDING A PARENT'S PERMISSION.

I DON'T FEEL COMFORTABLE GOING TO MY DOCTOR. DO I HAVE OTHER OPTIONS?

IF YOU'RE NOT COMFORTABLE SEEING YOUR REGULAR DOCTOR, YOU CAN CHECK OUT A HEALTH CLINIC INSTEAD. JUST SEARCH ONLINE FOR HEALTH CLINICS NEARBY OR CALL 211 (IN THE UNITED STATES) TO GET INFORMATION.

WILL MY PARENTS FIND OUT?

YOUR PARENTS WON'T FIND OUT UNLESS YOU WANT THEM TO. IT'S OKAY IF YOU DON'T FEEL LIKE TALKING TO THEM ABOUT GETTING CHECKED. UNLESS IT'S A LIFE-THREATENING SITUATION, YOU CAN GET TESTED PRIVATELY WITHOUT YOUR PARENTS KNOWING.

WHAT DOES IT COST?

THE PRICE OF GETTING TESTED WILL DEPEND ON WHERE YOU GO AND WHAT KIND OF TEST YOU NEED. SOMETIMES, PLACES LIKE HEALTH CLINICS OR NONPROFITS MIGHT GIVE YOU THE TEST FOR FREE OR AT A LOWER PRICE.

ROAD MAP TO STI TESTING*

START

FIND A HEALTH CLINIC

YOU CAN LOOK ONLINE OR CALL 211 (IN THE U.S.) TO BE CONNECTED TO LOCAL SERVICES.

MAKE AN APPOINTMENT

SOME CLINICS HAVE A TEXTING OPTION IF YOU'RE UNABLE TO CALL.

PLAN HOW YOU'LL GET THERE

FIND OUT HOW FAR IT IS FROM YOU AND TRANSPORTATION. IF YOU NEED SUPPORT, FIND A TRUSTED FRIEND OR ADULT TO GO WITH YOU.

BRING IMPORTANT DOCUMENTS

LIKE ID, INSURANCE CARDS, ETC.

SHARE INFORMATION

BE READY TO TALK ABOUT YOUR SEXUAL HISTORY.

GET TESTED

BE PREPARED TO EITHER PEE IN A CUP, GET A MOUTH SWAB, OR GET A BLOOD TEST.

BREATHE!

IF YOU HAVE AN STI, DON'T STRESS. MOST STI'S ARE CURABLE AND ALL ARE TREATABLE.

KNOW THAT YOU ARE **AWESOME** FOR STAYING ON TOP OF YOUR SEXUAL HEALTH!

REMEMBER: THE ONLY WAY TO COMPLETELY AVOID STI'S IS BY NOT HAVING SEX.

*ADAPTED FROM PLANNED PARENTHOOD

BARRIER METHODS

EXTERNAL CONDOMS

THESE TYPES OF CONDOMS COVER A PENIS. PEOPLE SOMETIMES CALL THIS A "MALE CONDOM."

HOWEVER, IT'S IMPORTANT TO NOTE THAT SOME WOMEN HAVE PENISES AND ALSO USE CONDOMS.

WHAT'S BETWEEN SOMEONE'S LEGS DOESN'T DETERMINE THEIR GENDER.

INTERNAL CONDOMS

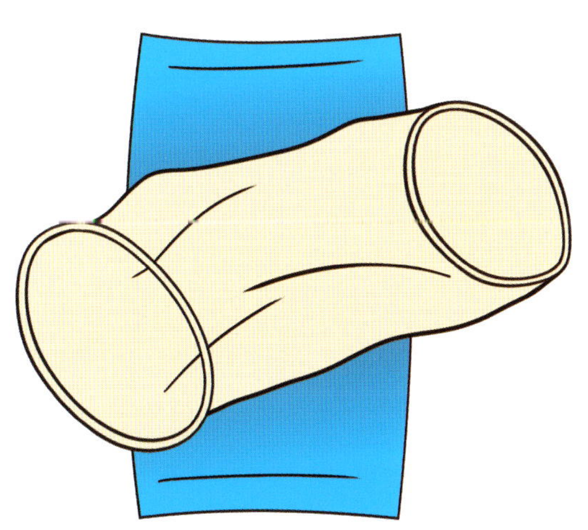

THIS CONDOM CAN GO INSIDE THE VAGINA OR ANUS.

INTERNAL CONDOMS HAVE NOTICEABLY LARGER SIZE AND SHAPE TO FIT THE INSIDE OF THE BODY.

YOU MIGHT HAVE HEARD THIS CALLED A "FEMALE CONDOM." BUT GUESS WHAT? IT'S NOT JUST FOR WOMEN! SOME GUYS HAVE A VAGINA TOO.

REMEMBER

IF SOMEONE WON'T USE A CONDOM, IT'S A CLEAR SIGN TO SAY "NO" TO SEX!

TURN TO PAGE 61 TO LEARN HOW CONDOMS ARE USED!

LUBRICANT

LUBE IS A PRODUCT THAT IS MEANT TO KEEP AN AREA OF THE BODY LUBRICATED AND COMFORTABLE.

WHEN SOMEONE APPLIES LUBE TO THE GENITALS, THIS REDUCES FRICTION AND MAKES THINGS SLIPPERY!

BODY PARTS THAT DO NOT SELF-LUBRICATE, LIKE THE ANUS, REQUIRE LUBE.

ANATOMY REMINDER: SENSITIVE NERVE ENDINGS AND TISSUE LINE THE ANUS.

LUBE PREVENTS ANY TEARING AND PROVIDES CUSHIONING INSIDE THE ANUS.

YOU CAN NEVER USE TOO MUCH LUBE!

IT'S ALSO IMPORTANT TO LOOK AT THE INGREDIENTS IN LUBE.

STAY AWAY FROM INGREDIENTS LIKE GLYCERIN AND PARABENS.

FOR VAGINA OWNERS WITH SENSITIVITIES, THIS CAN CAUSE IRRITATION.

RANDOM PORN FACT:

PORN PERFORMERS HAVE TO USE LUBRICANT IN MOVIES BECAUSE FILMING A COUPLE OF SEX SCENES CAN TAKE 10-12 HOURS!

HOW TO PUT ON AN EXTERNAL CONDOM

AFTER RECEIVING CONSENT

STEP 1

CHECK THE EXPIRATION DATE. YOU **DO NOT** WANT TO USE AN EXPIRED CONDOM. IT CAN TEAR EASILY AND MAY CONTAIN A BAD ODOR.

STEP 2

CHECK FOR AIR BUBBLES. IF THE WRAPPER IS FLAT, IT'S PUNCTURED IN SOME WAY.

THROW AWAY THE CONDOM AND GRAB A NEW ONE.

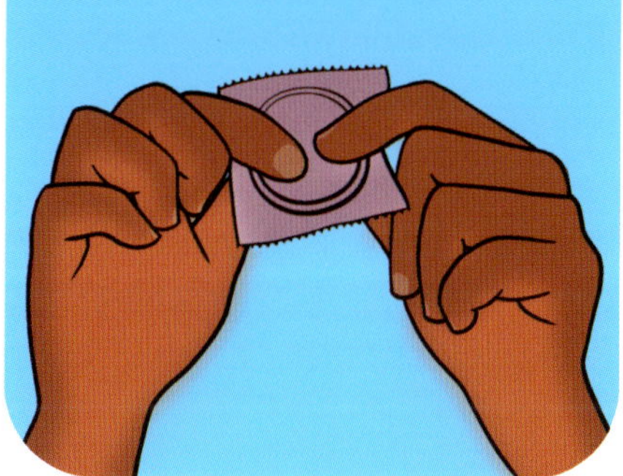

STEP 3

OPEN THE CONDOM WRAPPER BY TEARING IT FROM THE SIDE.

NEVER OPEN A CONDOM WITH YOUR TEETH BECAUSE THAT MAY RIP THE CONDOM.

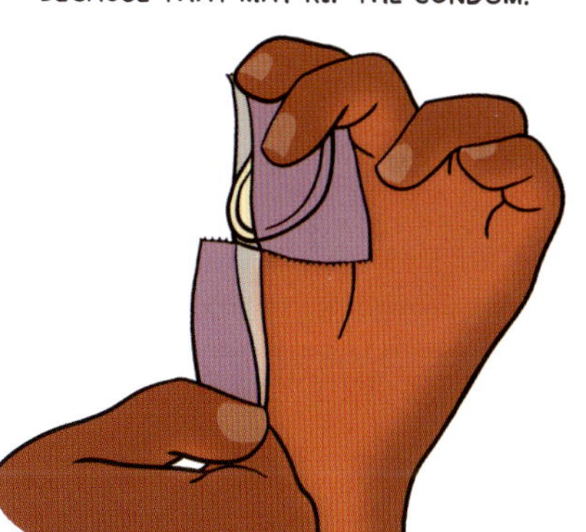

STEP 4

FIND OUT WHICH END GOES UP. YOU CAN DO THIS BY PUTTING THE CONDOM OVER YOUR FINGER AND ROLLING IT DOWN.

THERE IS ONLY ONE RIGHT WAY TO ROLL DOWN A CONDOM.

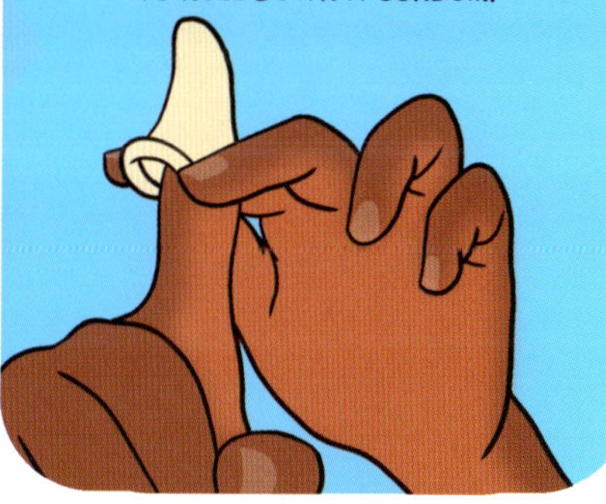

STEP 5

PINCH THE TIP OF THE CONDOM.

THIS WILL HELP KEEP SPACE AT THE TOP IN CASE SOMEONE EJACULATES.

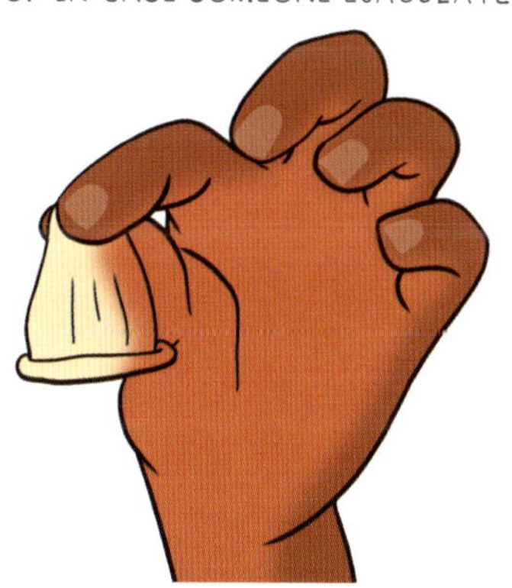

STEP 6

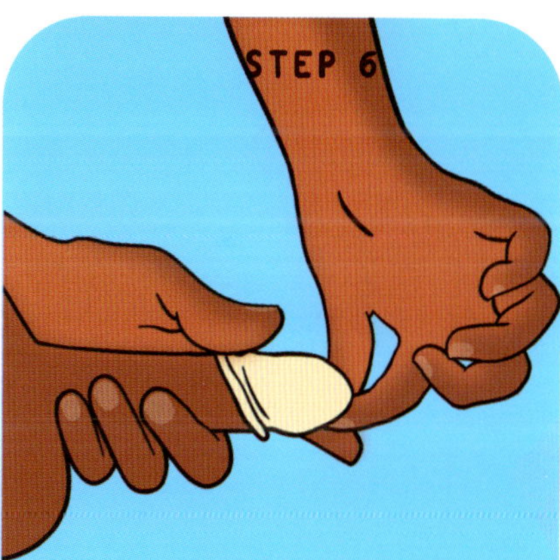

PLACE THE CONDOM OVER THE PENIS AND ROLL IT DOWN WHILE PINCHING THE TIP THE ENTIRE TIME.

STEP 7

ONCE SOMEONE IS FINISHED OR HAS EJACULATED, THEY WILL WANT TO MOVE AWAY FROM THEIR PARTNER AND SLOWLY ROLL THE CONDOM OFF.

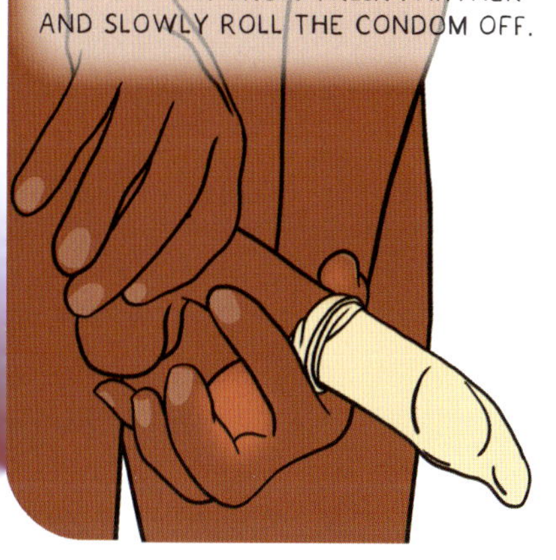

STEP 8

AFTER REMOVING THE CONDOM, TIE THE END IN A KNOT TO PREVENT FLUIDS FROM SPILLING. WRAP THE CONDOM IN A TISSUE AND THROW IT AWAY IN THE TRASH.

DO NOT FLUSH IT DOWN THE TOILET!

QUICK TIP

PLACE A FEW DROPS OF LUBRICANT INSIDE THE CONDOM BEFORE PUTTING IT ON.

THIS CAN INCREASE PLEASURE AND REDUCE ANY FRICTION.

HOW TO PUT ON AN INTERNAL CONDOM

AFTER RECEIVING CONSENT

STEP 1

CHECK THE EXPIRATION DATE. YOU **DO NOT** WANT TO USE AN EXPIRED CONDOM. IT CAN TEAR EASILY AND MAY CONTAIN A BAD ODOR.

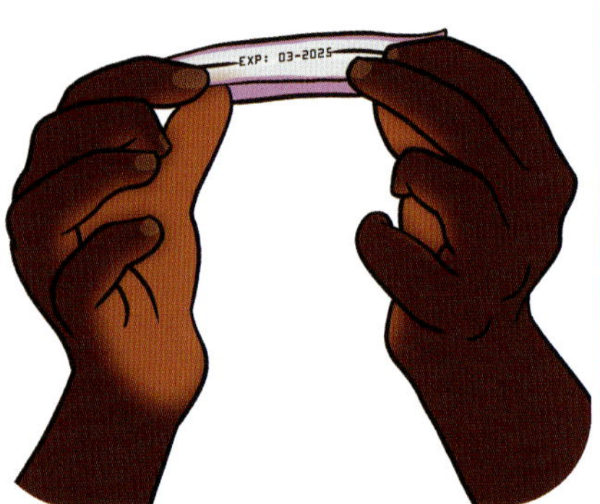

STEP 2

CHECK FOR AIR BUBBLES. IF THE WRAPPER IS FLAT, THAT MEANS IT'S PUNCTURED IN SOME WAY. THROW AWAY THE CONDOM AND GRAB A NEW ONE.

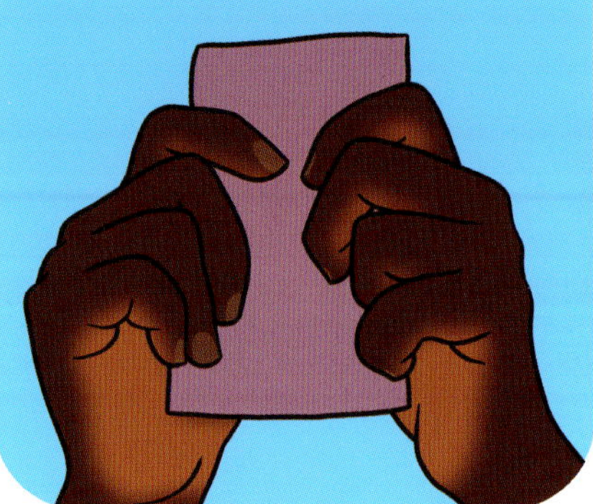

STEP 3

OPEN THE CONDOM WRAPPER BY TEARING IT FROM THE SIDE.

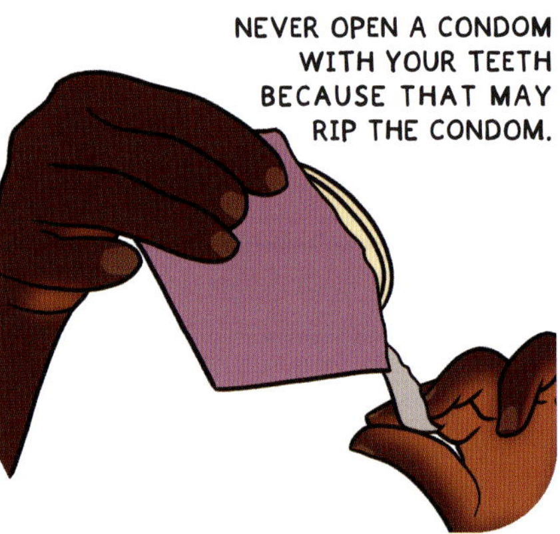

STEP 4

INSIDE THE CONDOM IS A FLEXIBLE RING.

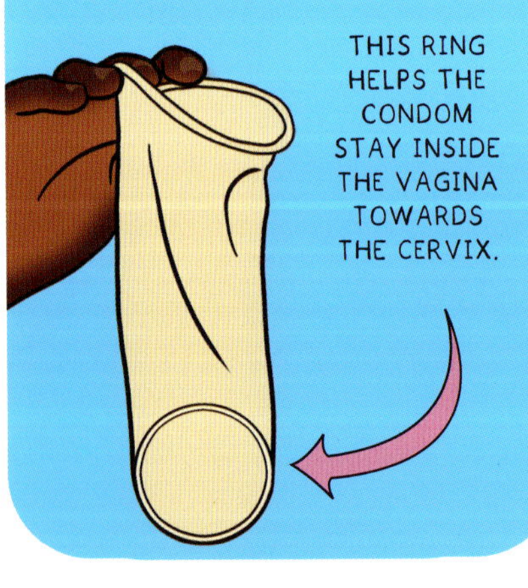

STEP 5

TAKE THE RING AND PINCH IT INTO A FIGURE-8.

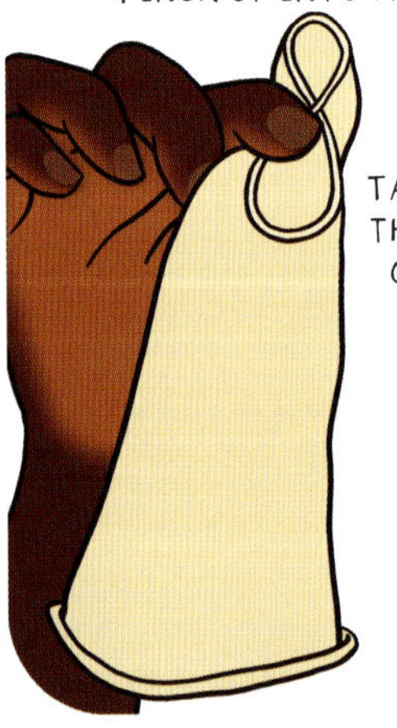

TAKE THIS END OF THE CONDOM AND GENTLY INSERT IT INTO THE VAGINA.

STEP 6

PUSH THE RING INSIDE THE BODY AS FAR AS POSSIBLE. THE CONDOM WILL STAY A LITTLE BIT OUTSIDE OF THE BODY TO COVER THE LABIA LIPS.

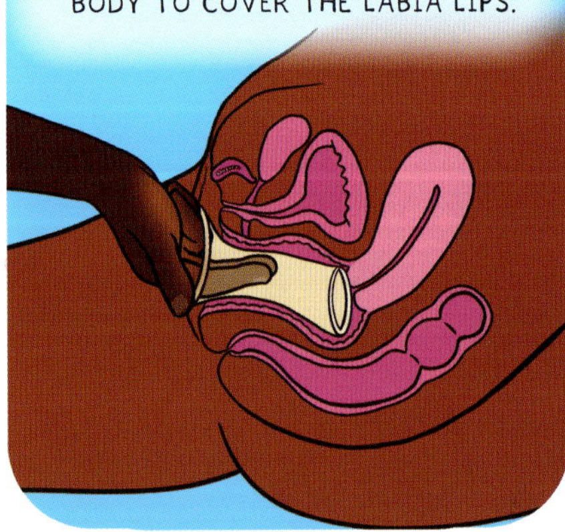

STEP 7

ONCE STIMULATION IS OVER, TWIST THE OUTER RING CLOCKWISE. **GENTLY** PULL THE CONDOM OUT OF THE BODY.

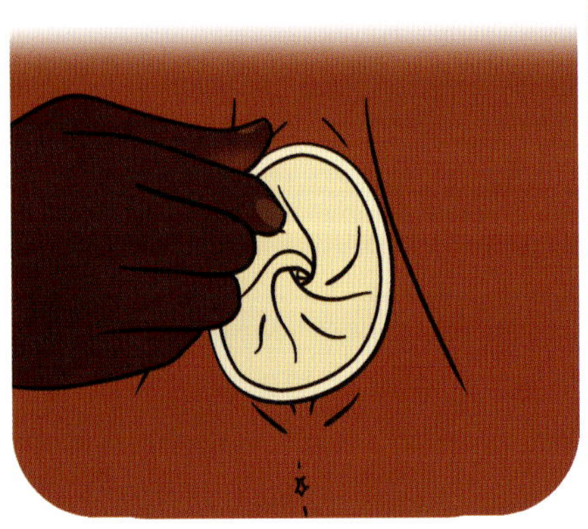

STEP 8

AFTER REMOVING THE CONDOM, TIE THE END IN A KNOT TO PREVENT FLUIDS FROM SPILLING. WRAP THE CONDOM IN A TISSUE AND THROW IT AWAY IN THE TRASH.

DO NOT FLUSH IT DOWN THE TOILET!

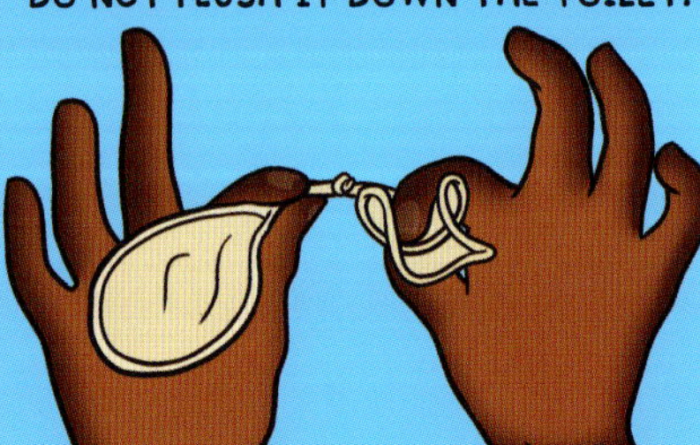

QUICK TIP

THE VAGINA CAN HAVE AN INTERNAL CONDOM INSIDE FOR UP TO 8 HOURS BEFORE PENETRATION.

HOW TO PUT ON AN INTERNAL CONDOM

FOR ANAL USE

STEP 1

CHECK THE EXPIRATION DATE. YOU **DO NOT** WANT TO USE AN EXPIRED CONDOM. IT CAN TEAR EASILY AND MAY CONTAIN A BAD ODOR.

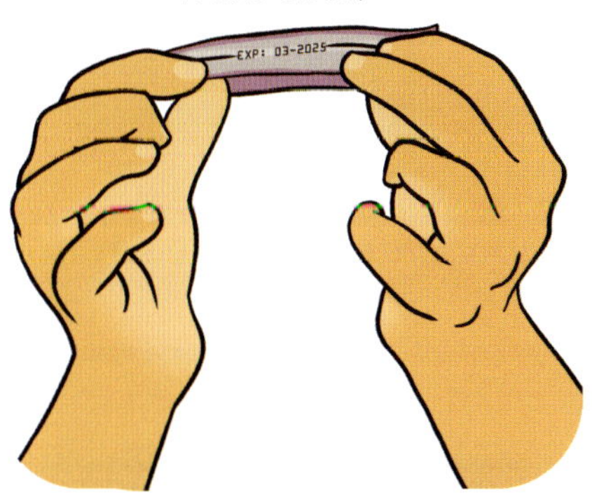

STEP 2

CHECK FOR AIR BUBBLES. IF THE WRAPPER IS FLAT, THAT MEANS IT'S PUNCTURED IN SOME WAY. THROW AWAY THE CONDOM AND GRAB A NEW ONE.

STEP 3

OPEN THE CONDOM WRAPPER BY TEARING IT FROM THE SIDE.

NEVER OPEN A CONDOM WITH YOUR TEETH BECAUSE THAT MAY RIP THE CONDOM.

STEP 4

REMOVE THE RING INSIDE OF THE CONDOM.

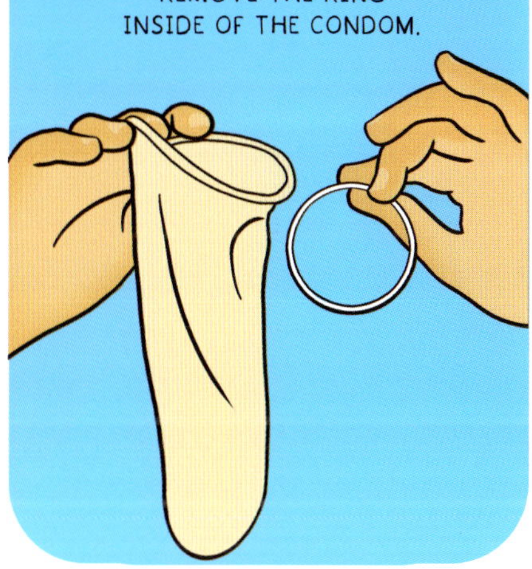

STEP 5

TAKE THE CONDOM AND PLACE IT ONTO A FINGER. NEXT, GENTLY INSERT IT INSIDE THE ANUS. APPLY LUBRICANT AS NEEDED.

STEP 6

PUSH THE CONDOM AS FAR AS YOU CAN INSIDE THE BODY. THE OUTER PART OF THE CONDOM WILL STAY OUTSIDE THE BODY.

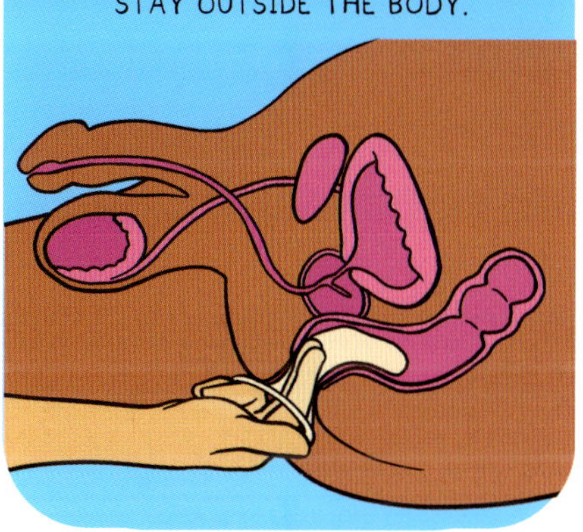

STEP 7

ONCE STIMULATION IS OVER, TWIST THE OUTER RING CLOCKWISE. **GENTLY** PULL THE CONDOM OUT OF THE BODY.

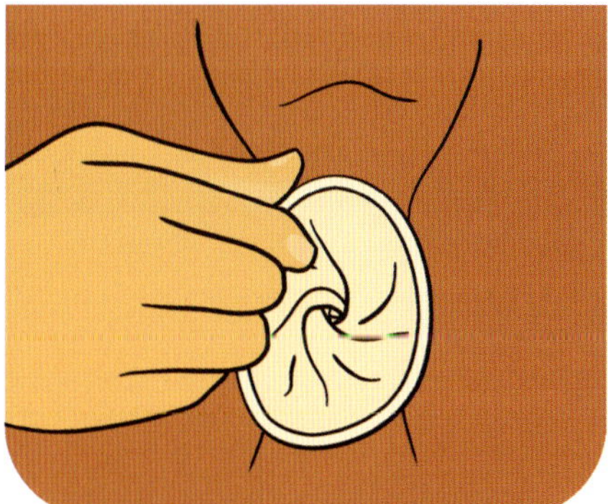

STEP 8

AFTER REMOVING THE CONDOM, TIE THE END IN A KNOT TO PREVENT FLUIDS FROM SPILLING. WRAP THE CONDOM IN A TISSUE AND THROW IT AWAY IN THE TRASH.

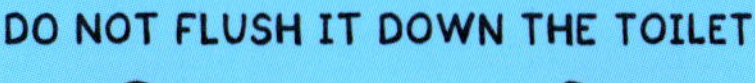

DO NOT FLUSH IT DOWN THE TOILET!

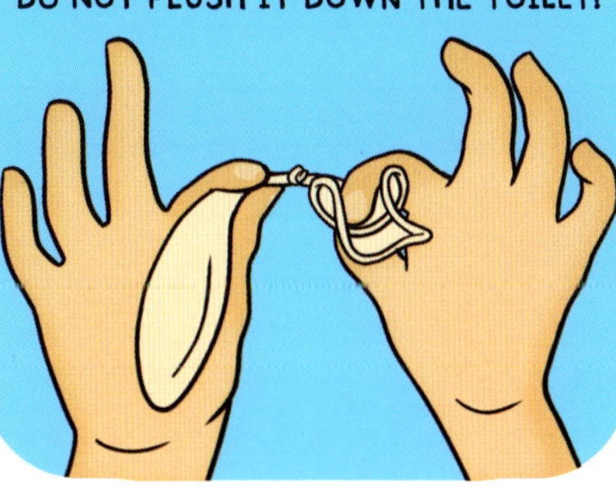

REMINDER

YOU CAN ONLY USE INTERNAL CONDOMS LIKE THIS BECAUSE THE OUTER RING ACTS AS A BASE, PREVENTING IT FROM FALLING INSIDE THE ANUS.

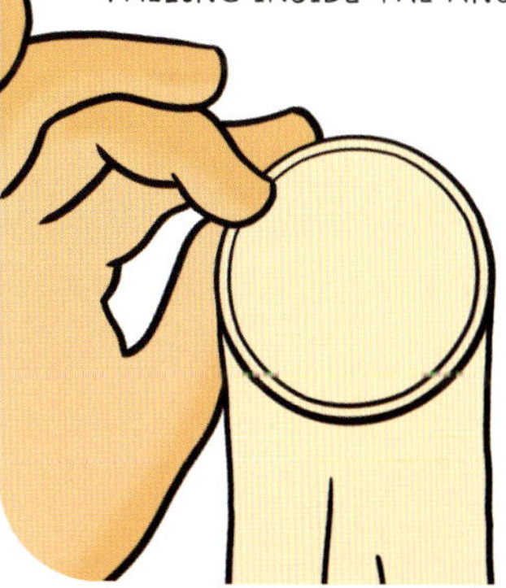

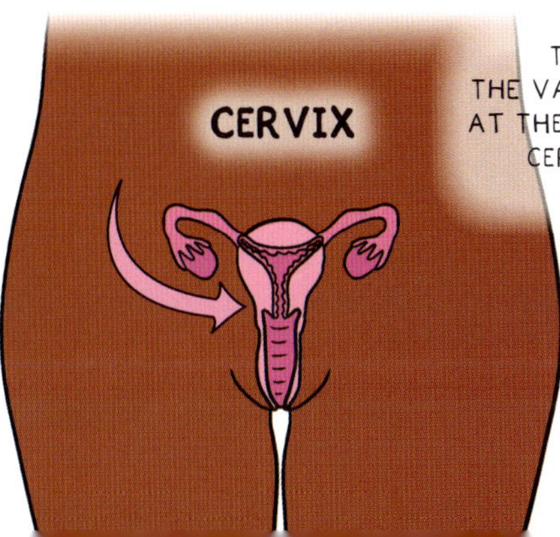

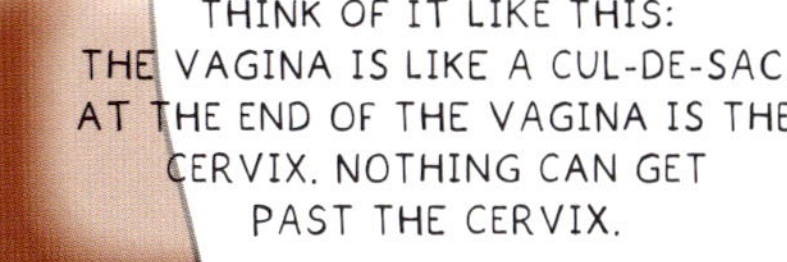

THINK OF IT LIKE THIS: THE VAGINA IS LIKE A CUL-DE-SAC. AT THE END OF THE VAGINA IS THE CERVIX. NOTHING CAN GET PAST THE CERVIX.

THE ANUS, HOWEVER, IS LIKE A ONE-WAY STREET IN WHICH THE COLON AND THE INTESTINES CONNECT. IF SOMETHING WERE TO FALL INTO THE ANUS (LIKE A CONDOM), IT WOULD GET STUCK, AND YOU MAY NEED TO GO TO A DOCTOR TO GET IT OUT!

COLON

HOW TO USE A DENTAL DAM

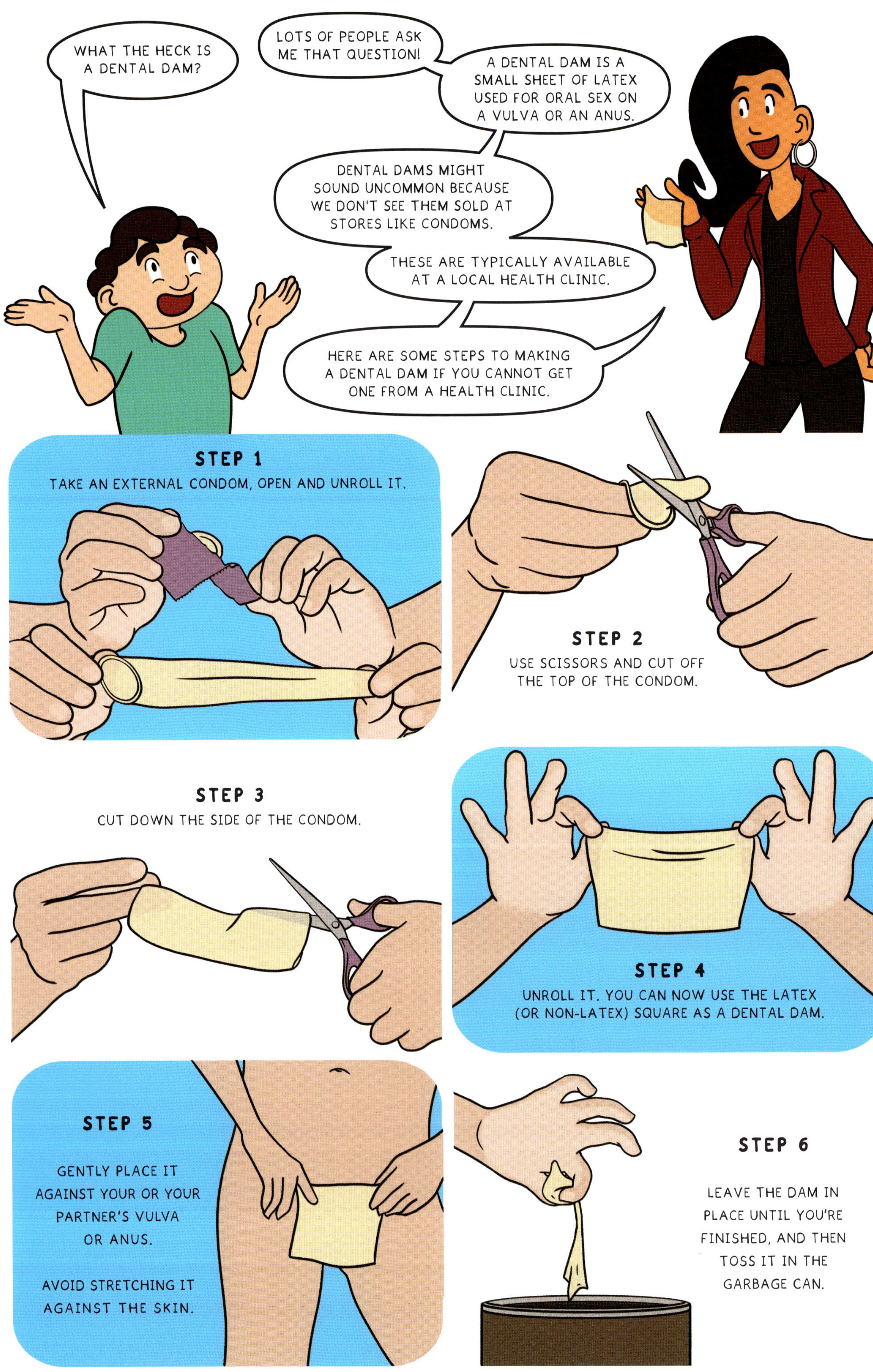

DENTAL DAMS USUALLY COME IN DIFFERENT FLAVORS LIKE STRAWBERRY, MINT, AND MORE!

LATEX AND NITRILE GLOVES
A CONDOM FOR YOUR WHOLE HAND! LATEX AND NITRILE GLOVES ARE A BARRIER METHOD FOR YOUR HAND. WHEN WE EXPLORE A PARTNER'S BODY, WE OFTEN START WITH OUR HANDS!
GLOVES HELP PROTECT FINGERS THAT MIGHT HAVE A CUT ON THEM.
THEY ARE ALSO GOOD FOR PEOPLE WHO HAVE LONG NAILS.
BE SURE TO ADD LUBE TO DECREASE ANY FRICTION AND INCREASE YOUR PLEASURE!
A QUICK TIP:
IF SOMEONE HAS ACRYLIC NAILS, THEY CAN PLACE COTTON BALLS IN EACH FINGER OF THE GLOVE. IT CAN HELP PROTECT THE GLOVE FROM BEING PUNCTURED BY THE NAIL.
FINGER COTS
INSTEAD OF A BARRIER METHOD FOR YOUR WHOLE HAND, FINGER COTS ARE SMALL CONDOMS FOR INDIVIDUAL FINGERS.
DURING SEX, SOMEONE MAY WEAR THESE FOR STIMULATION.
IF YOU HAVE EVER WATCHED COOKING SHOWS, YOU MIGHT SEE CHEFS WEARING THEM TO PROTECT THEIR FINGERS. YOU CAN PURCHASE FINGER COTS IN STORES WITH FIRST-AID AISLES, LIKE GROCERY STORES AND PHARMACIES.
NOT GONNA LIE, BUT GLOVES SOUND KINDA WEIRD.
THAT'S OKAY!
THESE TYPES OF BARRIERS ARE JUST SUGGESTIONS FOR SAFER SEX. EVERYONE IS DIFFERENT. YOU WILL KNOW WHAT WORKS BEST FOR YOU.

IMPORTANT THINGS TO REMEMBER

ONE AND DONE!

NEVER REUSE ANY BARRIER METHOD.

NEVER USE OIL-BASED PRODUCTS LIKE COCONUT OIL, LOTION, OR BABY OIL AS A LUBRICANT ON LATEX BARRIERS.

COCO NUT

NOT ONLY WILL THIS BREAK THE CONDOM OR DENTAL DAM, BUT THIS CAN ALSO GIVE SOME GENITALS AN INFECTION.

NO DOUBLE-BAGGING. USE ONE CONDOM AT A TIME.

PUTTING TWO CONDOMS ON A PENIS OR USING AN INTERNAL CONDOM AND EXTERNAL CONDOM AT THE SAME TIME WILL CAUSE FRICTION.

IT WILL WILL CAUSE THE CONDOM TO BREAK.

USING ONE CONDOM IS ENOUGH.

IF SOMEONE IS ALLERGIC TO LATEX, THERE ARE NON-LATEX CONDOMS AND GLOVES AVAILABLE.

THE INTERNAL CONDOM IS ALSO NON-LATEX.

THERE ARE SO MANY DIFFERENT TYPES OF CONDOMS. CONDOMS ARE LIKE SNOWFLAKES. EVERYONE HAS A PREFERENCE. ONE KIND OF CONDOM WILL NOT WORK FOR EVERYONE.

SAFER SEX CHECKLIST

TAKE A LOOK AT THESE LISTS AND CHECK OFF WHAT APPLIES TO YOU.

MATERIALS

I HAVE SAFER SEX SUPPLIES (CONDOMS, LUBE, ETC.)	YES	NO
I HAVE A BIRTH CONTROL METHOD	YES	NO
I KNOW WHERE MY NEAREST HEALTH CLINIC IS	YES	NO
I KNOW WHERE TO GET A PREGNANCY TEST	YES	NO
I KNOW WHERE TO GET TESTED FOR SEXUALLY TRANSMITTED INFECTIONS, INCLUDING HIV	YES	NO

BODY STUFF

MY PARTNER AND I KNOW OUR STI STATUS	YES	NO
I KNOW HOW MY BODY WORKS	YES	NO
I KNOW HOW MY PARTNER'S BODY WORKS	YES	NO
I KNOW WHEN MY BODY IS SEXUALLY AROUSED	YES	NO
I KNOW WHEN MY BODY IS UNCOMFORTABLE	YES	NO

EMOTIONAL STUFF

I KNOW WHY I WANT TO HAVE SEX	YES	NO
I HAVE SOMEONE TO TALK TO ABOUT SEX	YES	NO
I CAN HANDLE A POSSIBLE PREGNANCY OR INFECTION	YES	NO
I CAN HANDLE A POSSIBLE REJECTION OR BREAKUP	YES	NO
I KNOW MY LIMITS AND BOUNDARIES	YES	NO

RELATIONSHIP STUFF

I CAN TALK ABOUT SAFER SEX WITH MY PARTNER	YES	NO
I FEEL SAFE COMMUNICATING MY FEELINGS AND BOUNDARIES	YES	NO
MY PARTNER RESPECTS MY BOUNDARIES	YES	NO
I CAN TELL MY PARTNER WHAT FEELS GOOD	YES	NO
I KNOW WHAT'S BEST FOR ME	YES	NO

IF YOU HAVEN'T ANSWERED "YES" TO ALMOST EVERYTHING ON THE LIST, LOOK AT THE ONES YOU DIDN'T CHECK AND FIGURE OUT WHAT YOU NEED TO DO FOR YOURSELF RIGHT NOW.

THERE IS NO REASON TO RUSH INTO SOMETHING YOU ARE NOT READY FOR.

ALWAYS DO WHAT IS RIGHT FOR YOU.

REMEMBER, DURING SEXUAL EXPERIENCES, YOU CAN CHANGE YOUR MIND ANYTIME.

HOW DO YOU PUT ON A CONDOM?

TAKE A LOOK AT THE STEPS TO PUTTING ON AN EXTERNAL CONDOM. CUT OUT AND PLACE THE STEPS IN THE CORRECT ORDER. HOW FAST CAN YOU GO? CHALLENGE A FRIEND TO A TIMED RACE!

FIND THE CORRECT WAY TO ROLL DOWN THE CONDOM.	CHECK IN WITH YOUR PARTNER **DURING** THE SEXUAL ENCOUNTER.
PINCH THE TIP OF THE CONDOM AND PLACE IT ON THE HEAD OF THE PENIS.	ROLL DOWN THE CONDOM WHILE PINCHING THE TIP THE ENTIRE TIME.
GET A CONDOM AND CHECK THE EXPIRATION DATE.	HAVE SEXUAL ENCOUNTER.
PUSH THE CONDOM TO THE SIDE AND TEAR IT OPEN.	AFTER EJACULATION, MOVE AWAY FROM YOUR PARTNER AND SLOWLY ROLL THE CONDOM OFF.
COMMUNICATE WITH A PARTNER AND RECEIVE CONSENT.	TIE THE END OF THE CONDOM IN A KNOT AND THROW IT AWAY IN THE TRASH.
FEEL FOR AIR INSIDE THE CONDOM AND CHECK FOR ANY PUNCTURES.	PULL THE CONDOM OUT OF THE WRAPPER.
CHECK IN WITH YOUR PARTNER **AFTER** THE SEXUAL ENCOUNTER.	**BONUS CARD** PLACE A FEW DROPS OF LUBRICANT INSIDE CONDOM.

*ANSWERS IN BACK OF BOOK

CONVERSATION STARTER CARDS

CUT OUT AND FLIP THROUGH THESE CARDS WITH A PARTNER TO HELP FACILITATE A SAFER SEX TALK. YOU CAN EVEN TRY USING THESE CARDS TO REFLECT ON YOUR VALUES.

WHAT DO YOU CALL YOUR **GENITALS**?

WHAT SAFE WORD CAN WE USE TOGETHER IF WE FEEL LIKE WE **NEED TO STOP** OR HAVE A BREAK?

WHAT IS SOMETHING ABOUT SEX YOU HAVE ALWAYS WANTED TO **ASK ME**?

WHEN I GET **NERVOUS**, MY BODY RESPONDS BY...

WHAT DOES **EXPERIMENTING** MEAN TO YOU?

HAVE YOU USED **LUBRICANT** BEFORE? IF SO, WHAT KIND DO YOU LIKE?

HOW DO YOU FEEL ABOUT USING CONDOMS OR OTHER **BARRIER METHODS**?

DO YOU ALWAYS **USE PROTECTION**?

ARE YOU ON **BIRTH CONTROL**?

CAN I **KISS** YOU ON YOUR [*INSERT BODY PART*]?

DO YOU KNOW IF YOU HAVE ANY **STI'S**?

WHEN WAS THE LAST TIME YOU **TESTED** FOR STI'S? WHAT WAS YOUR RESULT?

DO YOU HAVE ANY OTHER SEXUAL **PARTNERS**?

HOW SHOULD WE **PRACTICE SAFER SEX** AND PREVENT STI'S?

DO YOU HAVE ANY **QUESTIONS** OR **CONCERNS** BEFORE WE ARE INTIMATE?

HAVE YOU EVER DISCUSSED SEXUAL **BOUNDARIES** WITH A PARTNER?

WHAT YOU NEED TO UNDERSTAND **ABOUT ME** AND SEX IS...

I PREFER TO **GIVE CONSENT** BY SAYING OR DOING...

ARE YOU **SEXUALLY ACTIVE**?

WOULD YOU LIKE TO GET **TESTED** AT THE CLINIC TOGETHER?

8

THIS CHAPTER WILL DISCUSS SENSITIVE INFORMATION ABOUT ASSAULT. IT MIGHT MAKE SOME PEOPLE UNCOMFORTABLE BECAUSE THESE TOPICS OFTEN COME UP IN PORN. REMEMBER, HAVING TOUGH CONVERSATIONS HELPS US BECOME MORE AWARE AND UNDERSTAND THESE ISSUES BETTER.

WHILE READING THIS CHAPTER, MAKE SURE TO HAVE A TRUSTED ADULT WITH YOU. IT'S IMPORTANT TO READ IT TOGETHER. THAT WAY, YOU CAN TALK OPENLY, ASK QUESTIONS, AND GET THE SUPPORT YOU NEED. HAVING A TRUSTED ADULT BY YOUR SIDE IS KEY TO KEEPING YOU SAFE AND FEELING COMFORTABLE AS YOU GO THROUGH THIS.

BEFORE WE BEGIN, I'D LIKE TO DEFINE THREE WORDS:
DOMINANCE POWER AND INFLUENCE OVER OTHERS.
AGGRESSION HOSTILE OR VIOLENT BEHAVIOR OR ATTITUDES TOWARDS OTHERS.
SEXUAL ASSAULT NON-CONSENSUAL SEXUAL INTERACTION.
IN PORN, THERE IS A FREQUENT PORTRAYAL OF MEN AS DOMINANT AND AGGRESSIVE.
SOMEONE CAN SHOW THIS PHYSICALLY
OR VERBALLY.
THEMES OF FORCE AND ASSAULT APPEAR IN SOME PORN, SHOWING WOMEN ENJOYING THIS MISTREATMENT.
THE PORN INDUSTRY REINFORCES THESE IDEAS.
HOWEVER, PORN IS NOT THE ONLY FORM OF MEDIA THAT INTRODUCES THIS IDEA.
UPDOG.333 3.3K POINTS
#METOO
REPLY SHARE REPORT
SIGMA-MIND 1042 POINTS - 14 HOURS
BOYS WILL BE BOYS
REPLY SHARE REPORT
USERNAME 101 POINTS
SAY LESS
REPLY SHARE
IN OUR SOCIETY, THERE IS SOMETHING CALLED **RAPE CULTURE**,
SHE WAS ASKING FOR IT
IF YOU DRESS LIKE THAT YOU KNOW WHAT WILL HAPPEN
...
VICTIM BLAMING
WHICH MEANS THAT DOMINANCE AND AGGRESSION TOWARD WOMEN ARE PRESENT AND NORMALIZED.
Teaching People to Avoid Sexual Assault vs. Teaching People to Not Sexually Assault
IT IS A CONCEPT THAT COMES FROM MAKING SEXUAL ASSAULT SEEM NORMAL, AND IT HAPPENS BECAUSE OF HOW SOCIETY THINKS ABOUT GENDER AND SEXUALITY.
WE SEE EXAMPLES OF THIS AGAIN IN ADVERTISEMENTS AND OTHER FORMS OF MEDIA.
I DON'T GET IT. WHY DOES RAPE CULTURE EXIST?
DOES THIS ONLY HAPPEN TO GIRLS?
RAPE CULTURE SILENCES AND MINIMIZES SURVIVORS OF SEXUAL ASSAULT. SEXUAL ASSAULT CAN HAPPEN TO PEOPLE OF ANY AGE AND GENDER.
WE MUST RECOGNIZE WHAT RAPE CULTURE IS SO WE CAN EDUCATE OTHERS AND PREVENT IT FROM HAPPENING.

SEXUAL ASSAULT IS A WIDESPREAD ISSUE IN THE UNITED STATES.

THE FOLLOWING STATISTICS REVEAL ITS IMPACT ON INDIVIDUALS AND COMMUNITIES.

THIS IS SOMETHING THAT HAPPENS MORE THAN WE THINK IT DOES. YOU ARE DESERVING OF SAFETY, LOVE, AND AN ADULT YOU CAN TRUST.

1 IN 4 GIRLS, and

1 IN 13 BOYS

IN THE UNITED STATES EXPERIENCE SEXUAL ABUSE.

4x

TRANSGENDER PEOPLE ARE MORE LIKELY THAN CISGENDER PEOPLE TO EXPERIENCE SEXUAL ABUSE.

91% OF SEXUAL ABUSE IS DONE BY SOMEONE THE VICTIM KNOWS.

SOURCE: NATIONAL CENTER FOR INJURY PREVENTION AND CONTROL, DIVISION OF VIOLENCE PREVENTION, 2023

REMEMBER, PORN IS PORTRAYED AS A **FANTASY**.

CONVERSATIONS ABOUT BOUNDARIES AND CONSENT HAPPEN BEHIND THE SCENES.

PORN PERFORMERS ARE ACTING OUT A SCENE KNOWING THAT IT WILL OR WILL NOT CONTAIN A FORM OF AGGRESSION AND DOMINANCE.

AFTER PERFORMERS FINISH THESE TYPES OF SCENES, THEY CHECK IN WITH EACH OTHER TO MAKE SURE EVERYONE IS OKAY.

ONE THING TO REMEMBER ABOUT MEDIA, INCLUDING PORN, IS THE **TARGETED AUDIENCE**.

THIS TYPE OF PORN INTENDS TO CAPTURE THE AUDIENCE OF **STRAIGHT MEN**.

REFER BACK TO CHAPTER 2, WHEN WE DISCUSSED THE MALE GAZE IN THE MEDIA.

WHY IS IT IMPORTANT TO UNDERSTAND PORN AS FANTASY, NOT REALITY?

ASK YOUR ADULT

WHAT ADVICE DO YOU HAVE IF I SEE OR HEAR SOMEONE MAKING INAPPROPRIATE COMMENTS ABOUT CONSENT OR SEXUAL ASSAULT?

HOW CAN I ADDRESS THESE SITUATIONS?

WHAT SHOULD I DO IF I EVER FEEL SCARED OR UNCOMFORTABLE WITH PEOPLE, AND WHO CAN I TALK TO FOR HELP?

BOUNDARIES

BOUNDARIES ARE RULES OR LIMITS A PERSON CREATES TO PROTECT THEIR ENERGY **MENTALLY, EMOTIONALLY,** AND **PHYSICALLY.**

WHEN YOU SET A BOUNDARY, YOU PRIORITIZE YOURSELF, YOUR NEEDS, AND YOUR VALUES. BOUNDARIES TEACH OTHERS HOW YOU WANT AND DESERVE TO BE TREATED.

HERE ARE THREE DIFFERENT WAYS TO DEFINE PERSONAL BOUNDARIES:

PHYSICAL BOUNDARIES

PERSONAL SPACE

HOW SOMEONE IS ALLOWED TO TOUCH YOU *(HUGGING, KISSING)*

WHO IS ALLOWED TO TOUCH YOU *(BEST FRIEND, ROMANTIC PARTNER)*

WHERE AND WHEN SOMEONE CAN TOUCH YOU *(HOLDING HANDS IN PUBLIC)*

SEXUAL BOUNDARIES

HOW SOMEONE IS ALLOWED TO TALK TO OR TEXT YOU SEXUALLY

WHO CAN TOUCH YOU SEXUALLY, AND WHEN

WHERE SOMEONE CAN TOUCH YOU SEXUALLY

THE LIMITS OF YOUR SEXUAL OR NON-SEXUAL ACTIVITY

EMOTIONAL BOUNDARIES

THE PEOPLE WHO YOU FEEL COMFORTABLE TALKING TO ABOUT PERSONAL THINGS

SOMEONE YOU SHARE YOUR SECRETS WITH

SOMEONE YOU CAN FEEL VULNERABLE WITH

LETTING OTHERS KNOW WHEN YOU NEED SPACE

HERE ARE SOME EXAMPLES OF PERSONAL BOUNDARIES:

Talk about personal stuff

Ask about my sexual orientation

Invite to your house

Send memes

Kiss

Saying "I Love You"

Texting

Shaking hands with someone

Holding hands

Give a hug

Using pronouns

WHAT ARE SOME OF THE BOUNDARIES THAT YOU HAVE?

____

____

____

HOW MIGHT YOU REACT IF SOMEONE CROSSES YOUR BOUNDARIES? WHAT WOULD BE YOUR BEST OUTCOME?

____

____

____

ASK YOUR ADULT

WHEN YOU WERE MY AGE, HOW DID YOU FIRST LEARN ABOUT SETTING BOUNDARIES?

DID YOU EVER FEEL UNSURE ABOUT SETTING BOUNDARIES WITH FRIENDS OR FAMILY MEMBERS?

REMEMBER:

YOU ARE *NOT* RESPONSIBLE FOR OTHER PEOPLE'S REACTIONS WHEN YOU SET BOUNDARIES.

YOU ARE PUTTING THEM IN PLACE TO PROTECT YOURSELF AND YOUR ENERGY. IF SOMEONE HAS AN ISSUE WITH THAT, THAT IS *ON THEM.*

9

THIS CHAPTER WILL DISCUSS STAYING SAFE WHILE USING DIFFERENT FORMS OF MEDIA, INCLUDING PORNOGRAPHY. IT'S IMPORTANT TO NOTE THAT THIS BOOK DOESN'T ASSUME YOU'RE VIEWING PORNOGRAPHY BUT PROVIDES GUIDANCE IF YOU ENCOUNTER IT OR OTHER RISKY MEDIA.

REMEMBER, FIND YOUR TRUSTED ADULT IF YOU EVER FEEL UNCOMFORTABLE OR NEED SUPPORT.

ONCE YOU COMPLETE THIS CHAPTER, FIND YOUR TRUSTED ADULT TO TALK TO AND ASK ANY QUESTIONS YOU HAVE.

MEDIA LITERACY

ACCESS:

HOW, WHEN, AND WHERE YOU GET THE INFORMATION FROM

ANALYZE:

ASK QUESTIONS ABOUT THE MEDIA YOU USE

EVALUATE:

MAKE YOUR OWN CONCLUSION ABOUT THE MEDIA YOU USE

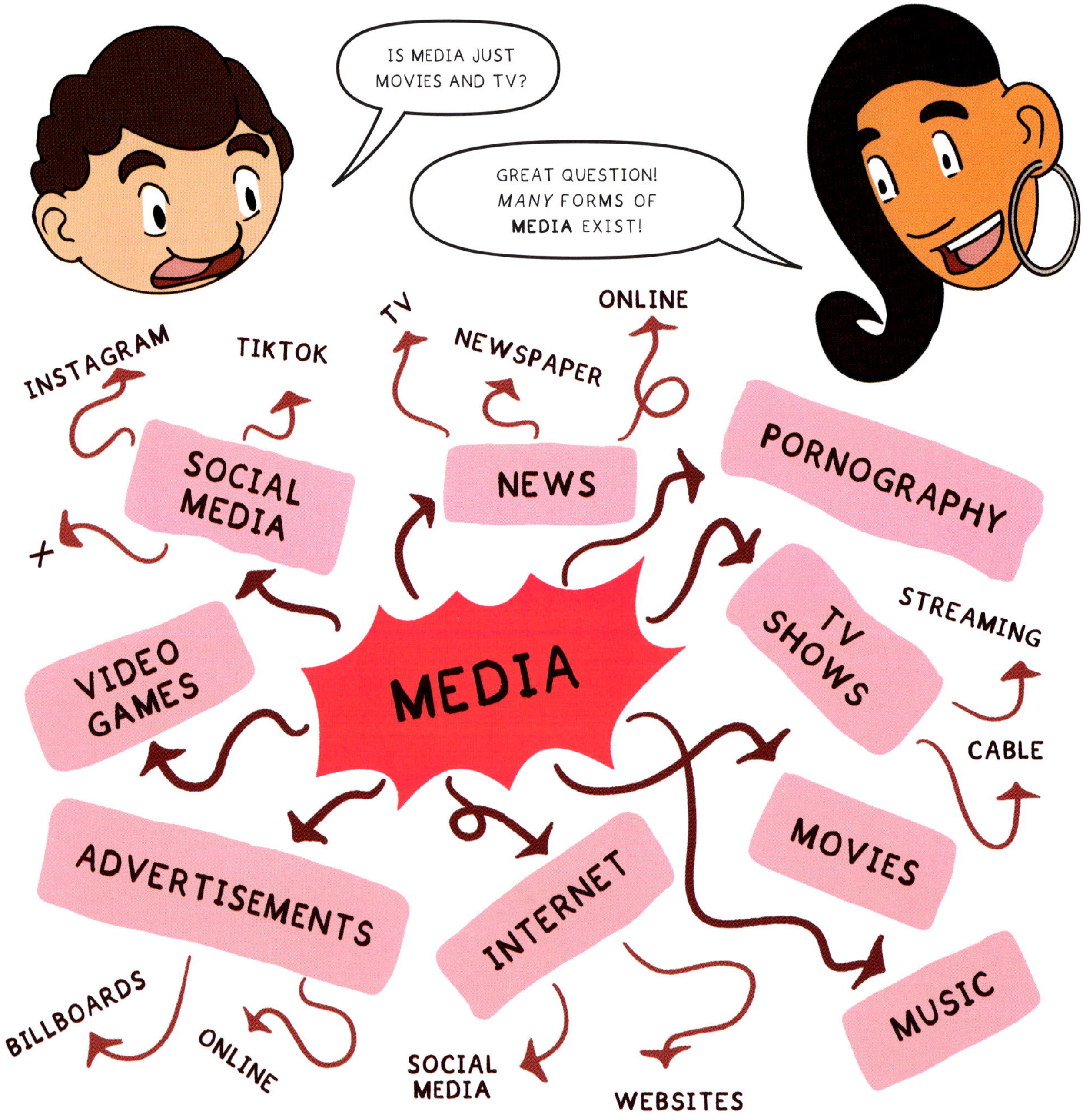

IS MEDIA JUST MOVIES AND TV?

GREAT QUESTION! *MANY* FORMS OF **MEDIA** EXIST!

MEDIA

SOCIAL MEDIA: INSTAGRAM, TIKTOK, X

NEWS: TV, NEWSPAPER, ONLINE

PORNOGRAPHY

TV SHOWS: STREAMING, CABLE

MOVIES

MUSIC

INTERNET: SOCIAL MEDIA, WEBSITES

ADVERTISEMENTS: BILLBOARDS, ONLINE

VIDEO GAMES

WRITE DOWN ANY FORMS OF MEDIA THAT YOU THINK MIGHT BE MISSING ABOVE.

MEDIA LITERACY IS A PROCESS WHERE WE (THE VIEWER) LEARN HOW TO ASK QUESTIONS ABOUT THE MEDIA WE SEE TO UNDERSTAND IT BETTER.

HERE ARE SOME QUESTIONS TO ASK YOURSELF WHEN VIEWING MEDIA:

TEENS? WOMEN?

WHO IS THIS MESSAGE INTENDED FOR?

LGBTQIA+ FOLKS?

LISTENING TO MUSIC?

WHERE DID I SEE THIS MESSAGE?

IN A MOVIE? ONLINE?

CLOTHES MAKE-UP

IS THIS MESSAGE TRYING TO SELL ME SOMETHING?

TECHNOLOGY

ACCEPT THESE MESSAGES OR REJECT THEM ENTIRELY

PORN LITERACY

THE MAIN GOAL OF PORN LITERACY IS KNOWING THAT:

PORN IS NOT TO REPLACE SEXUAL EDUCATION.

ABSTINENCE
CHOOSING NOT TO WATCH PORN IS ANOTHER OPTION.
IF PORN MAKES SOMEONE UNCOMFORTABLE, THEY CAN DECIDE NOT TO WATCH IT.

NOT VIEWING PORNOGRAPHY CAN ELIMINATE MIXED MESSAGES ABOUT SEX AND SEXUALITY.

CHOOSING NOT TO WATCH CERTAIN TYPES OF PORN CAN ALSO HELP SOMEONE FIGURE OUT WHAT THEY ARE COMFORTABLE WATCHING AND UNCOMFORTABLE WITH.
XXX

NO ONE SHOULD FEEL PRESSURED INTO WATCHING SOMETHING THEY DO NOT WANT TO.
REMEMBER, PORN IS A FORM OF ENTERTAINMENT FOR ADULTS FOR A REASON.

10

CONCLUSION

YAY, YOU DID IT!
YOU NOW KNOW MORE ABOUT PORN LITERACY THAN SOME ADULTS DO!

USE THIS LAST CHAPTER AS A GUIDE TO REFLECT ON YOUR LEARNING EXPERIENCE. DISCUSS WITH YOUR TRUSTED ADULT TO GAIN VALUABLE INSIGHTS TOGETHER.

REFLECTION QUESTIONS

WRITE DOWN SOMETHING NEW YOU LEARNED ABOUT SEX AND RELATIONSHIPS.

WRITE DOWN TWO THINGS THAT YOU THINK ALL TEENS SHOULD KNOW ABOUT SEX AND RELATIONSHIPS.

1)

2)

WHAT DO YOU THINK ALL TEENS SHOULD KNOW ABOUT PORNOGRAPHY?

IF A YOUNG PERSON (SIBLING, COUSIN, NEIGHBOR, ETC.) ASKED YOU ABOUT PORN, WHAT INFORMATION WOULD YOU SHARE WITH THEM?

WHAT ELSE HAVE YOU LEARNED WHILE READING THIS BOOK?

WHO IS A TRUSTED ADULT YOU CAN GO TO FOR QUESTIONS ABOUT SEX AND SEXUALITY? WHY DID YOU CHOOSE THIS PERSON?

WHAT DO WE DO NOW?

WHILE READING THIS BOOK, YOU MIGHT HAVE NOTICED THAT IT DIDN'T TELL YOU WHAT YOU *SHOULD* OR *SHOULDN'T* DO. THE PURPOSE OF THIS BOOK WAS TO **KEEP YOU INFORMED** ABOUT WHAT IS OUT THERE IN THE MEDIA. DURING YOUR LIFETIME, YOU WILL ENCOUNTER DIFFERENT MESSAGES IN *MOVIES*, *MUSIC*, *SOCIAL MEDIA*, AND *PORN*. WHETHER OR NOT YOU CHOOSE TO BE A PORN CONSUMER IS UP TO YOU.

THIS BOOK HAS GIVEN YOU THE TOOLS TO **IDENTIFY WHAT PORN IS** – A FORM OF ENTERTAINMENT *FOR ADULTS,* AND NOT A MEDICALLY ACCURATE FORM OF SEXUAL HEALTH EDUCATION. REMEMBER, IT'S NORMAL TO BE CURIOUS ABOUT SEX AND SEXUALITY. IT'S ALSO IMPORTANT TO *UNDERSTAND THE DIFFERENCE* BETWEEN SEXUAL **REALITY** AND SEXUAL **FANTASY**. HAVING THIS INFORMATION HELPS US LEARN HOW TO COMMUNICATE WITH OTHERS AND IDENTIFY HEALTHY RELATIONSHIPS. JUST THINK, SOME ADULTS ARE UNAWARE OF HALF OF THE INFORMATION YOU NOW HAVE!

PORN LITERACY IS ABOUT ASKING QUESTIONS AND IDENTIFYING HOW PORN RELATES TO YOUR LIFE. YOU CAN TAKE THIS INFORMATION AND SHARE IT WITH THOSE WHO YOU FEEL MAY NEED IT *(WHICH IS ANYONE REALLY)*. YOU'RE PRACTICALLY A PORN LITERACY EXPERT NOW! ALSO, THINK ABOUT *THE ADULTS IN YOUR LIFE*. WHO CAN YOU COMFORTABLY ASK QUESTIONS ABOUT SEX AND SEXUALITY WITH (MAYBE EVEN THE PERSON WHO GIFTED YOU THIS BOOK)? **IF YOU NEED MORE INFORMATION, LOOK AT THE BACK OF THE BOOK FOR ADDITIONAL SEXUAL HEALTH RESOURCES.**

YOU GOT THIS!

GLOSSARY

ASEXUALITY: SOMEONE WHO EXPERIENCES LITTLE TO NO SEXUAL ATTRACTION TOWARDS INDIVIDUALS OF ANY GENDER. AN ASEXUAL PERSON CAN STILL DESIRE AN EMOTIONAL AND ROMANTIC CONNECTION WITH OTHERS.

BREAST: IN ANATOMY, THIS IS A MAMMARY GLAND THAT EXTENDS FROM THE FRONT OF THE CHEST. AFTER PREGNANCY, THESE CAN PRODUCE MILK TO FEED A BABY.

CIRCUMCISION: A SURGERY IN WHICH THE FORESKIN IS CUT FROM THE PENIS, EXPOSING THE TIP; DONE FOR PERSONAL, RELIGIOUS, OR CULTURAL REASONS.

CISGENDER: A PERSON WHOSE GENDER IDENTITY ALIGNS WITH THEIR BIOLOGICAL SEX (E.G., A PERSON ASSIGNED MALE AT BIRTH GROWS UP AND IDENTIFIES AS A MAN).

CLITORIS: A HIGHLY SENSITIVE GLAND ON THE VULVA MADE OUT OF ERECTILE TISSUE THAT CAN BE ERECT DURING AROUSAL.

COMMUNICATION: HAVING A CONVERSATION WITH SOMEONE WHERE VIEWPOINTS ARE EXPRESSED TO EACH OTHER. PEOPLE CAN COMMUNICATE THEIR THOUGHTS, EMOTIONS, AND DESIRES.

CONDOM: A SAFER SEX BARRIER THAT CAN PROTECT AGAINST SEXUALLY TRANSMITTED INFECTIONS AND PREGNANCY; APPLIES TO INTERNAL CONDOMS (INSIDE THE ANUS OR VAGINA) AND EXTERNAL CONDOMS (ON A PENIS).

CONSENT: HAVING PERMISSION TO DO SOMETHING FROM EVERY PERSON INVOLVED (E.G., A HUG, A CONVERSATION, A KISS).

EJACULATION: (FOR PENISES) WHEN SEMEN, USUALLY ABOUT 1-2 TEASPOONS, COMES OUT OF AN ERECT PENIS. (FOR VULVAS) WHEN A CLEAR FLUID IS RELEASED FROM THE URETHRA DURING OR BEFORE AN ORGASM.

EXPLOITATION: THE ACT OF MISTREATING SOMEONE IN ORDER TO BENEFIT FROM THEIR WORK; TAKING ADVANTAGE OF SOMEONE ELSE.

FANTASY: THE ACTIVITY OF IMAGINING SITUATIONS THAT ARE UNLIKELY, UNREALISTIC, OR IMPOSSIBLE.

GAY: TERM USED TO DESCRIBE MALE-IDENTIFIED PEOPLE ATTRACTED ROMANTICALLY, EROTICALLY, AND EMOTIONALLY TO OTHER MALE-IDENTIFIED PEOPLE; A TYPE OF SEXUAL ORIENTATION.

GENDER IDENTITY: ONE'S INTERNAL SENSE OF BEING MALE, FEMALE, NEITHER OF THESE, BOTH, OR ANOTHER GENDER; CAN BECOME COMPLEX AND IS BETTER UNDERSTOOD AS A SPECTRUM.

GENDER ROLES: CULTURAL NORMS AND EXPECTATIONS OF HOW PEOPLE OF A SPECIFIC GENDER ACT, OFTEN BASED ON STEREOTYPES. ALSO KNOWN AS "GENDER NORMS."

GLAMORIZE: TO MAKE SOMEONE OR SOMETHING SEEM MORE ATTRACTIVE OR EXCITING THAN IT IS.

HETERONORMATIVE: THE SOCIETAL ASSUMPTION THAT EVERYONE IS HETEROSEXUAL AND THAT HETEROSEXUALITY IS SUPERIOR TO OTHER SEXUALITIES; SEE HETEROSEXUAL.

HETEROSEXUAL: A WORD TO DESCRIBE SOMEONE PHYSICALLY AND EMOTIONALLY ATTRACTED TOWARD PEOPLE OF THE OTHER BINARY GENDER; USED INTERCHANGEABLY WITH THE WORD "STRAIGHT"; A TYPE OF SEXUAL ORIENTATION.

HUMAN TRAFFICKING: A CRIME INVOLVING SOMEONE USING FORCE, FRAUD, OR COERCION TO BENEFIT FROM SOMETHING ANOTHER PERSON DOES; INCLUDES SEX AND LABOR TRAFFICKING.

INTERSEX: HAVING REPRODUCTIVE ORGANS, GENITALS, HORMONES, OR CHROMOSOMAL PATTERNS THAT DO NOT FALL UNDER TYPICAL DEFINITIONS OF MALE AND FEMALE.

LESBIAN: A WOMAN WHO IS SEXUALLY OR ROMANTICALLY ATTRACTED TO OTHER WOMEN; TYPE OF SEXUAL ORIENTATION.

LGBTQIA+: A COMMON ABBREVIATION FOR LESBIAN, GAY, BISEXUAL, TRANSGENDER, QUEER, INTERSEX, ASEXUAL, AND OTHER IDENTITIES; DESCRIBING A COMMUNITY.

LUBRICANT: A SAFER SEX PRODUCT USED ON THE GENITALS TO INCREASE WETNESS, CUSHION, AND HEIGHTEN PLEASURE.

MAINSTREAM: THE IDEAS REGARDED AS NORMAL OR CONVENTIONAL; THE DOMINANT TREND IN OPINION, FASHION, OR MEDIA.

MALE GAZE: HOW THE MEDIA PORTRAYS WOMEN AS OBJECTS OF MALE PLEASURE.

MASTURBATION: WHEN SOMEONE SAFELY EXPLORES THEIR OWN BODY FOR PLEASURE.

MISOGYNY: THE DISLIKE OR HATRED OF WOMEN AND GIRLS.

NIPPLE: IN ANATOMY, THE SMALL RAISED AREA IN THE MIDDLE OF A BREAST; BREAST MILK WILL FLOW THROUGH THIS AREA AFTER PREGNANCY.

PENIS: BODY PART WHERE URINE AND SEMEN EXIT THE BODY; FILLED WITH PLEASURE-SENSITIVE NERVE ENDINGS.

PLEASURE: REFERS TO EXPERIENCES THAT MAKE US FEEL GOOD AND WE ENJOY. FOR EXAMPLE, THE COMFORT YOU EXPERIENCE FROM TAKING A WARM BATH.

PORNOGRAPHY: ANY WRITTEN, VISUAL, OR OTHER MEDIA DESIGNED TO SEXUALLY EXCITE ADULTS (18 AND OLDER).

QUEER: A PERSON WHOSE SEXUAL ORIENTATION OR GENDER IDENTITY FALLS OUTSIDE THE HETEROSEXUAL MAINSTREAM OR THE GENDER BINARY; ONCE USED AS A SLUR, IT HAS BEEN RECLAIMED BY MANY AS AN EMPOWERING IDENTITY.

RACISM: DISCRIMINATION AND PREJUDICE AGAINST PEOPLE BASED ON THEIR RACE OR ETHNICITY.

REALITY: THE WORLD AS IT EXISTS; OPPOSITE OF FANTASY.

SAFER SEX: TOOLS TO PREVENT SEXUALLY TRANSMITTED INFECTIONS, AVOID UNWANTED PREGNANCIES, AND INCREASE HEALTHY RELATIONSHIPS.

SEXUAL ASSAULT: SEXUAL CONTACT OR BEHAVIOR THAT HAPPENS WITHOUT CLEAR CONSENT FROM THE OTHER PERSON.

SEXUAL HEALTH EDUCATION: INFORMATION ABOUT HOW OUR BODIES CHANGE, SEX, SEXUALITY, AND RELATIONSHIPS. PROVIDES SKILLS ON HOW TO COMMUNICATE AND MAKE HEALTHY CHOICES FOR OUR SEXUAL HEALTH.

SEXUAL ORIENTATION: A PERSON'S ROMANTIC, EMOTIONAL, PHYSICAL, OR SEXUAL ATTRACTION TO ANOTHER PERSON.

SEXUALITY: A PERSON'S EXPLORATION OF SEXUAL IDENTITY, GENDER, AND SEXUAL ORIENTATION.

SEXUALLY EXPLICIT: NON-CENSORED MATERIAL THAT PRESENTS SEXUAL CONTENT.

SEXUALLY TRANSMITTED INFECTION (STI): AN INFECTION THAT IS TRANSMITTED THROUGH SEXUAL CONTACT.

SEX ASSIGNED AT BIRTH: A PERSON'S BIOLOGICAL COMBINATION OF HORMONES, ORGANS, GENITALS, AND CHROMOSOMES; REFERS TO DOCTORS CLASSIFYING PEOPLE AS MALE, FEMALE, AND INTERSEX.

SEX (BEHAVIOR): SEXUAL ACTIVITY DONE ALONE OR WITH ANOTHER PERSON; A UNIQUE DEFINITION THAT MEANS SOMETHING DIFFERENT TO EVERYONE.

SEX-POSITIVE: A SHAME-FREE AND NON-JUDGMENTAL SET OF VALUES TOWARDS YOUR SEXUALITY AND OTHERS.

SEX WORK: THE CONSENSUAL AND MONETARY EXCHANGE BETWEEN ADULTS (18 OR OVER) OF SEXUAL SERVICES, PERFORMANCES, OR PRODUCTS; ONLY LEGAL IN CERTAIN PARTS OF NEVADA (UNITED STATES).

SPERM: THE MALE REPRODUCTIVE SEX CELL.

STEREOTYPE: A PRECONCEIVED OR OVERSIMPLIFIED GENERALIZATION ABOUT AN ENTIRE GROUP OF PEOPLE WITHOUT REGARD FOR THEIR INDIVIDUAL DIFFERENCES.

STI STATUS: WHETHER SOMEONE IS DIAGNOSED WITH A SEXUALLY TRANSMITTED INFECTION OR NOT.

SYMPTOM: PHYSICAL SIGNS THAT MIGHT INDICATE AN INFECTION.

TABOO: SOMETHING DETERMINED BY SOCIETY AS IMPROPER OR UNACCEPTABLE.

TRANSGENDER: TERM TO DESCRIBE A PERSON WHOSE GENDER IDENTITY IS DIFFERENT FROM THEIR SEX ASSIGNED AT BIRTH; A TYPE OF GENDER IDENTITY.

URETHRA: THE TUBE THAT CONNECTS THE BLADDER TO THE OUTSIDE OF THE BODY; WHERE URINE AND SPERM EXIT FROM THE PENIS.

VAGINA: STRETCHY, MUSCULAR PASSAGE CONNECTING THE UTERUS AND VULVA; WHERE MENSTRUAL BLOOD FLOWS OUT OF THE BODY.

VAGINAL FLUIDS: A CLEAR OR WHITISH FLUID THAT COMES OUT OF THE VAGINA; THE WALLS OF THE VAGINA CAN LUBRICATE AND CREATE FLUIDS WHEN SEXUALLY EXCITED.

VULVA: THE EXTERNAL GENITALS COMBINED; INCLUDES THE LABIA LIPS, CLITORIS, URETHRA, AND VAGINA.

ACTIVITY ANSWERS

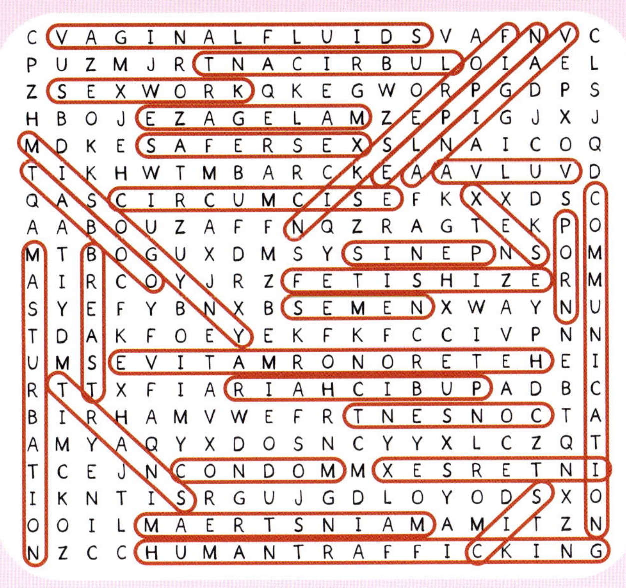

CH 1, PG 11

NORMALIZING SEX

WORD SEARCH PUZZLE

CH 4, PG 37

ANATOMY

CROSSWORD

CH 7, PG 68

HOW DO YOU PUT ON A CONDOM?

SEXUAL HEALTH RESOURCES

SCAN HERE FOR MORE INFORMATION ON:

OR GO TO: WWW.REALTALKWITHJESS.COM/SEXUAL-HEALTH-RESOURCES

A NOTE TO PARENTS AND TRUSTED ADULTS

HEY THERE, FELLOW ADULT! HIGH-FIVE FOR BEING OPEN TO UNDERSTANDING PORN LITERACY WITH YOUR TEEN! HAVING THESE CONVERSATIONS IS ESSENTIAL, AND I'M GLAD YOU'RE HERE TO LEARN AND NAVIGATE THIS TOPIC TOGETHER.

BEFORE YOU DIVE INTO THE BOOK, LET'S BE HONEST. THIS CONVERSATION CAN BE DIFFICULT FOR SOME OF US, AS MANY HAVE DIFFERENT FEELINGS TOWARD PORNOGRAPHY. THIS BOOK INTENDS TO INITIATE THIS DISCUSSION USING A NON-JUDGMENTAL APPROACH. YOUNG PEOPLE ARE GOING TO BE CURIOUS ABOUT SEX AND SEXUALITY. WHEN YOU'RE THERE TO SUPPORT THEM, THEY'LL FEEL COMFORTABLE COMING TO YOU WITH ANY QUESTIONS. JUST REMEMBER, IT'S ALL ABOUT KEEPING THE LINES OF COMMUNICATION OPEN AND BEING THERE FOR EACH OTHER!

THIS BOOK WILL HAVE PROMPTS MEANT TO ENCOURAGE YOUR YOUNG PERSON TO REACH OUT TO YOU TO DISCUSS THE TOPIC. USE THIS OPPORTUNITY TO SHARE YOUR VIEWPOINTS AND INSIGHTS.

DOES THAT MAKE YOU NERVOUS? LET'S RE-FRAME THIS: THE FACT THAT YOUR YOUNG PERSON IS REACHING OUT TO YOU WITH QUESTIONS SHOWS THAT THEY HAVE IDENTIFIED YOU AS A TRUSTED ADULT. TAKE THIS TIME TO OFFER SUPPORT IN A SHAME-FREE WAY.

ASK YOURSELF:

QUESTIONS FOR ADULTS TO REFLECT ON

HOW COMFORTABLE DO YOU FEEL TALKING ABOUT SEX AND SEXUALITY?

WHAT MESSAGES ABOUT PORN DID YOU RECEIVE AS A YOUNG PERSON?

HOW DO YOU WANT TO BE AN ALLY AND SUPPORT THE YOUNG PEOPLE IN YOUR LIFE?

HERE ARE THREE TIPS FOR DISCUSSING PORN WITH YOUR YOUNG PERSON:

VALIDATE CURIOSITY

AS A YOUNG PERSON GROWS AND BECOMES CURIOUS ABOUT SEX, REMEMBER THAT IT'S A NORMAL PART OF LIFE, AND IT'S OKAY TO HAVE OPEN CONVERSATIONS ABOUT IT. ENCOURAGE THEM TO COME TO YOU WITH THEIR QUESTIONS OR CONCERNS. REMIND THEM THAT WATCHING PORN TO LEARN ABOUT SEX WILL NOT GIVE THEM AN ACCURATE UNDERSTANDING.

BE HONEST

YOU DON'T HAVE TO BE A SEX WIZARD TO ANSWER ANY QUESTIONS ABOUT PORN. IF YOU'RE UNSURE OF A QUESTION, LET THEM KNOW. YOU CAN RESEARCH TOGETHER TO FIND THE ANSWER AND SHARE YOUR VIEWPOINTS. THIS WAY, YOU CAN LEARN AND EXPLORE TOGETHER, FOSTERING TRUST AND UNDERSTANDING IN YOUR RELATIONSHIP.

EMPHASIZE THAT PORN IS FICTION

PORN IS AN UNREALISTIC DEPICTION OF SEX AND SEXUALITY.

PORN IS A FORM OF ENTERTAINMENT CREATED FOR ADULTS FOR A REASON. FIND ADDITIONAL AGE-APPROPRIATE RESOURCES *(E.G., THIS BOOK)* TO EXPLAIN SEX AND SEXUALITY TO YOUR CHILD BETTER.

AS TRUSTED ADULTS, WE PLAY A CRUCIAL ROLE IN PROVIDING ACCURATE INFORMATION AND GUIDANCE, ENSURING THAT YOUNG PEOPLE FEEL SUPPORTED AND EMPOWERED TO MAKE INFORMED DECISIONS AS THEY NAVIGATE THEIR UNDERSTANDING OF SEX AND SEXUALITY. THROUGH THESE CONVERSATIONS, WE CAN FOSTER TRUST AND STRENGTHEN OUR ADULT-CHILD RELATIONSHIP, ULTIMATELY HELPING YOUNG PEOPLE DEVELOP INTO CONFIDENT AND RESPONSIBLE INDIVIDUALS.

YOU GOT THIS!

THANK YOU TO **MARLENE** FOR BEING MY FOREVER HYPE WOMAN.

A FOR BEING MY INSPIRATIONAL MENTOR AND BELIEVING IN ME.

S FOR OFFERING YOUR EXPERTISE AND SUPPORT.

LOVE YOU ALL!!